Walking the Tyne

Twenty-five Walks

From mouth

To source

J.B.Jonas

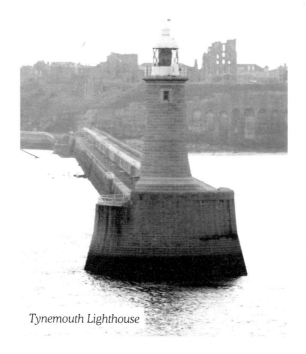

Tynemouth Lighthouse

First Edition   February 2001

Second Edition   May 2002

Third Edition   July 2004

Printed by Abbey Press, Priestpopple, Hexham, Northumberland

ISBN 1 901184 70 6

Contents

Acknowledgements

We would not be able to walk the paths in this book were it not for the efforts of the many organisations who maintain and signpost them and whose offices have been invariably helpful and encouraging when I have contacted them. I am most grateful.

I am extremely grateful to Nick Lord of Mowden Hall School, who has translated my handwritten maps into the printed versions you see in the book and has done all the typing and layout. Without his skill and enthusiasm this book would not have been possible.

I would also like to thank my wife Mary and son James for walking most of the walks with me and for their patience as I took notes and reconnoitred alternative routes.

All the maps are based on the Ordnance Survey 1:25000 Explorer 316 Map (Newcastle upon Tyne / Blaydon & Prudhoe) and Outdoor Leisure 31 (North Pennines) and 43 (Hadrian's Wall) and are reproduced from Ordnance Survey mapping on behalf of Controller of Her Majesty's Stationery Office © Crown Copyright MC 0100030976.

James Jonas

The Ramblers' Association

This book is published by the Ramblers' Association – Northern Area. The publishers cannot be held responsible for errors of omissions in the text and while we have endeavoured to point out difficult sections of route, safety is an individual's own responsibility.

The Ramblers' Association promotes walking as a healthy activity for all ages. It seeks to protect Rights of Way and to open up new and disused ones. It campaigns for Access to Open Country and seeks to preserve our countryside.

Your local R.A. contact will be listed in the phone directory – or write to the R.A. Head Office at Camelford House, 87-90 Albert Embankment, London SE1 7TW.

Follow the Country Code

Ann Key (Vice Chair, Northern R.A.)

Preface

There are many books and leaflets, which describe walks at or near some stretches of the River Tyne, but none, which covers the whole length of the River from mouth to source. This book does just that and gives the reader the choice of short or long distance walks. The whole way is a linear walk of 85 miles, which experienced long distance walkers will find they can fit comfortably into a week's holiday (see below), but each of the 25 individual walks, most of them circular, cover the whole river too, so, as my wife and I did with the Weardale Way, you can complete the route at intervals to suit yourself.

The Tyne splits into North and South Tynes just west of Hexham, from where onwards this is, strictly, the South Tyne walk. Why this route? The North Tyne valley is beautiful and should be explored, but there are far fewer stretches of riverside path, Kielder Reservoir has obliterated the river for many miles and beyond the reservoir it seems to peter out. Does it start as Deadwater Burn or Bell's Burn? The map gives no clue. The South Tyne on the other hand runs, uninterrupted, from its source on Tynehead Fell all the way to the sea.

Why also you might ask, from mouth to source? Most river walks follow that direction; because their mouths tend to be well known, often harbour towns and villages, whereas there is often mystery (even today) about the source. Exploring the Tyne one's sense of adventure is heightened as one starts in the city, moves through the pastoral central section and completes the walk in the high Pennines, England's last wilderness.

The walk must of course follow Rights of Way, and there is no continuous riverside path. Where there is a suitable path beside the

Collingwood Monument

Tyne this walk will follow it, but a good walk has varied scenery and terrain, and, although we are almost always in the Tyne Valley, the walk may in places be a mile or two from the river, if that is the prettiest – or more challenging way to go.

Note on the Second and Third Editions

The Second and Third Editions have given the opportunity to clarify some of the directions and correct the occasional textual error, but the majority of the First Edition walks remain unchanged and all can still be walked almost as described. However, one or two developments since have allowed what I think are rather better versions of sections of Walks 1, 3, 5 and 25. The Right of Way between Fourstones and Laverick Planation has been rerouted, so I have revised the map. Some other maps have had minor revisions. Some extra stiles and footbridges have been built between Miles 78 and 79 (Walk 23). I have not revised the map as the route is very clear. Negotiations to reinstate the section of path near Farnley Scar (Walk 10) are nearly completed. Hopefully the rerouted path will be open during the currency of this edition (see pages 30 and 32).

How to use the book

Individual walks: 17 of the 25 walks are circular, i.e. a 'round' starting and finishing in the same place (see page 3). Walk 25 to the source is part circular and part linear. The other 4 are one-way (linear) but all in areas with frequent public transport back to the start; 3 could be either linear or circular

Each walk is accompanied by a detailed map and full description of the route, but it is a good idea to take Ordnance Survey maps as well, for a wider picture of the countryside around you.

The 'vital statistics' (distance, time, terrain, car parking, refreshments) are given for each walk and more general information about public transport and accommodation later in this introduction.

The long distance walker from mouth to source, should follow the outward leg of each individual walk – clear instructions are given as to where you continue from one walk to the next. Further guidance is provided by the mileage on each map for the linear walk and more prominent heads on the maps' directional arrows.

Experienced walkers know their own capabilities so I have not presumed to put in any suggested timings. However, it may be helpful to know that there are Youth Hostels in Newcastle, at Acomb (2 miles north of Hexham – reasonable bus service), Greenhead (2 miles west of Haltwhistle – hourly buses) and Alston. Based on these the Tyne could easily be walked in a week allowing two days for travel to and from the Tyne and 5 days of walking.

Suggested stages could be:

Stage	Walks	Miles
Tynemouth – Newcastle (or Newburn)	1 to 3 (or 5)	15 (or 21)
Newcastle – Hexham (or Newburn)	3 (or 5) to 11	25 (or 19)
Hexham – Haltwhistle	12 to 16	20 (22 via Warren Hse)
Haltwhistle – Alston	17 to 22	14
Alston – the Source & return	23 to 25	18 inc. the return

Accommodation

Details from local Tourist Offices in North / South Shields, Gateshead, Newcastle, Corbridge, Hexham, Haltwhistle and Alston. Youth Hostels - see section on Long Distance Walkers - above.

Public Transport

Walks 1 – 5: Transport details given for each walk.

Walks 4 – 17: are accessible by -

Weekdays

Train: Newcastle, Gateshead (Metro Centre), Wylam, Prudhoe, Stocksfield, Riding Mill, Corbridge, Hexham – hourly, and to Hexham, Haydon Bridge, Bardon Mill, Haltwhistle, Carlisle – roughly hourly.

Bus: Newcastle, Wylam, Ovingham, Ovington – Go Ahead 684 hourly.

Newcastle, Prudhoe, Stocksfield, Riding Mill, Corbridge, Hexham – Arriva 602 half-hourly.

Newcastle, Corbridge, Hexham, Haydon Bridge, Bardon Mill, Haltwhistle, Carlisle – Arriva/Stagecoach 685 hourly.

Hexham, Fourstones, Newbrough – Tyne Valley 10 daily.

Walks 18 – 25: Very few buses between Haltwhistle and Alston. Essential to check beforehand. Beyond Alston there is currently no suitable transport.

Sundays: fewer trains and buses run – see local timetables

Maps

Most maps are to scale (1:25000) but some liberties have been taken with the scale where page size is a constraint.

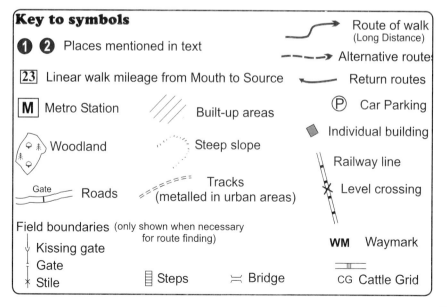

Key to symbols

❶ ❷ Places mentioned in text

➤ Route of walk (Long Distance)

- - -➤ Alternative routes

23 Linear walk mileage from Mouth to Source

◄— Return routes

M Metro Station

/// Built-up areas

Ⓟ Car Parking

Woodland

Steep slope

▪ Individual building

Gate Roads

Tracks (metalled in urban areas)

Railway line

✗ Level crossing

Field boundaries (only shown when necessary for route finding)

Kissing gate

Gate

Stile

Steps

⊨ Bridge

WM Waymark

CG Cattle Grid

Walk 1: Tynemouth to South Shields (linear or circular)

A kaleidoscope of the River Tyne

This walk provides a fascinating view of the busy river and fishing port – and includes trips on the ferry. The distance from Mouth to Source is measured from North Shields Pier, which is the recommended route, though you can start at South Shields Pier and join the walk at mile 3 (see below). Walk 1's suggested route is North Shields Pier (Car Park) – Fish Quay – Ferry – River Drive – Arbeia Fort – North Marine Park – Ocean Road (for Museum) – South Shields Market – Ferry and return to start, if doing the circular walk.

To start at the very mouth of the Tyne walk out to North Pier Lighthouse, where you may be rewarded with a close-up view of vessels entering or leaving the river. The pier is open during daylight hours except in rough seas. Head back to shore under the imposing ruins of **Tynemouth Castle** and **Priory (1)**, turn left onto Pier Road, past the **Watch House Museum (2)**, (closed on Mondays) onto the pedestrian only Promenade – part of the Waterside Trail. Climb the grassy slope on your right to inspect the **Admiral Collingwood Monument (3)**. Returning to the Promenade you pass the **Black Midden Rocks** which claimed 34 victims in 1864 when 5 ships were wrecked in blizzards – so close to shore. The Promenade leads through the fish warehouses to the **Fish Quay (4)**, home port of the North Shields fishing fleet. Follow Union Street, past a host of fishmongers displaying freshly caught fish at tempting prices. Count the Fish and Chip shops too! After Union Quay keep on the same road following the line of the river, past some new buildings, to end at **New Quay (5)**. Turn left down to the Ferry Landing (Ferry currently departs on the hour and half hour) for the crossing to **South Shields Ferry Landing (6)**. Purists might like to walk up and down on the Ferry too! Long distance walkers should now continue on Walk 2, though you might like to pause a while to visit the **Market (12)**, the excellent **Museum (11)**, especially if you are a Catherine Cookson fan, and **Arbeia Roman Fort (10)**, with its impressive reconstructed Gateway, Barrack Block and Commander's House.

To continue Walk 1 turn left after leaving the Ferry Landing along **Riverside Walkway (7)**, turn right at the now flooded former dry dock to come to a main road. Turn left and follow this road until, at a series of black bollards, it becomes **Wapping Street (8)**. Almost at once climb steep steps to your right. When you come to a metalled path turn right then almost at once left up a further flight of steps. Cross the grassy area and follow River Drive, shortly crossing over and following **Greens Place (9)** to reach Arbeia Roman Fort. Turn left into Fort Street (Note Aurelian and Valerian Terraces!) and cross Lawe Road into North Marine Park. Various paths lead you to Ocean Road, which takes you past the **Museum (11)**, and the **Market (12)** to the Ferry.

An alternative starting point to the long distance walk would be the South Pier lighthouse. Returning along the Pier you would cross the main (Sea) road, turn right into North Marine Park. Traverse the Park to reach Arbeia. Follow River Drive,

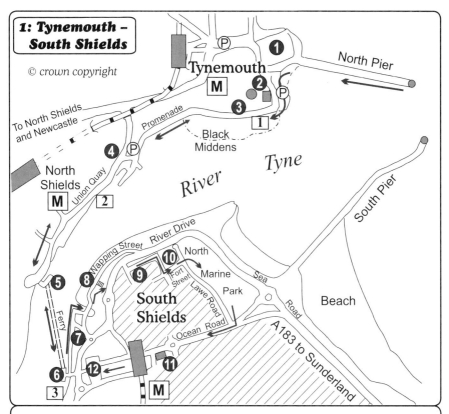

1: Tynemouth – South Shields

© crown copyright

Distance: 5 miles (8 km) to South Shields Metro +3 more if returning to Tynemouth

Time: 3 hours (plus ferry crossing, sight seeing), or 4½ hours for the complete 'round', including return ferry

Longer distance walkers might consider North Shields to Pelaw (for Metro) – 11 miles or to Newcastle Swing Bridge (15 miles)

Terrain: Metalled paths, pavements, 2 flights of steps

Transport: Tyne and Wear Metro [M] to Tynemouth or South Shields Stations.

Buses from much of SE Northumberland and Arriva Bus 306 from Newcastle (Haymarket) to Tynemouth Front Street. Buses from North Shields Ferry. Frequent buses from Sunderland, South Tyneside, County Durham to South Shields Market Place. Go Ahead Bus 310 Sunderland & Jarrow to Tynemouth.

Car Parking: as shown in Tynemouth – Fish Quay is free. Several car parks in South Shields.

Refreshments: wide choice on Quayside (plenty of fish!), and South Shields.

Start: see text for choices

(which, being high above the river, gives good river views) round to South Shields town centre, and Market Place to join the route from North Shields at the Ferry landing. On balance, though, I would recommend the North Shields start, with a diversion to Arbeia after the Ferry crossing.

Walk 2: South Shields to Jarrow or Hebburn (linear)

'Ancient and modern'. This is the only walk which involves a substantial amount of pavement beside busy roads, but not only is there always something to see in the many glimpses of the river with its ship repairing yards and commercial traffic, but you also go back in time a couple of centuries at Mill Dam and into the First Millennium at Bede's Jarrow. You can also cross under the Tyne and back through the (free) Pedestrian Tunnel. Those not walking on towards Newcastle might wish to omit the least interesting Jarrow to Hebburn stretch.

Distance: South Shields to Jarrow (Metro) 4½ miles (7 km) *Time*: 2½ hours.
    South Shields to Hebburn (Metro) 6½ miles (10 km) *Time*: 3½ hours.
Transport: Metro back to South Shields or Bus 527 Jarrow (Bus Sta.) and Bede's World (not Hebburn) to South Shields.
Car Parks: South Shields, Bede's World, Jarrow (Ellison Street), and Hebburn (near Metro).
Refreshments: Bede's World and a number of pubs 'en route'.
Start: South Shields ferry landing

From **South Shields Ferry landing (1)** turn right onto the new Riverside promenade to **Corporation Quay (2)** with fine views of the river. Walk round the **Customs House**, now restored as a cinema, theatre and restaurant, turn right, cross the car park to the left hand end of the muraled wall then right up the service road in front of Riverside Court (see Inset Map) to a flight of steps leading back to Commercial Road. Turn right. The diversion round **Nile Street (3)** affords impressive views of shipyard cranes, ship repairing and metal casting works, survivors of the great days of Tyne shipbuilding and heavy engineering. A second loop along Laygate Street (not signed, but turn into it at Jennings Car Sales) and **West Holborn (4)** affords further glimpses of the river and perhaps of the Scandinavian Ferries at the **International Ferry Terminal** opposite. You rejoin Commercial Road, which now becomes Temple Town. The picturesque three storied houses of **Thornton Avenue (5)** built in 1890, with their wooden bow fronts in many different colours, remind one of San Francisco. The Tyne Dock Pub displays one of the many impressive inn signs depicting the docks and quays which you pass by en route. Keep right at the roundabouts along the A194 and A185. This is an uninspiring stretch of road unless you risk the higher narrow roadside path when it diverges from the main footpath, as that allows you views across Tyne Dock and Jarrow Slake to the old and new Tyneside developments. The walk continues through

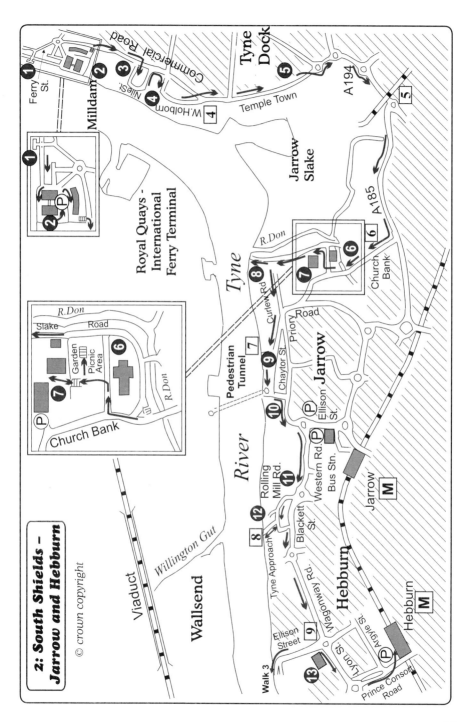

2: *South Shields –*
Jarrow and Hebburn

© crown copyright

Ferry St.

Milldam

Commercial Road

Nile St.

W. Holborn

Temple Town

Tyne Dock

A194

Jarrow Slake

Royal Quays - International Ferry Terminal

River Tyne

R.Don

R.Don

Slake Road

Garden

Picnic Area

Church Bank

A185

Church Bank

Priory Road

Curlew Rd.

Pedestrian Tunnel

Chaytor St.

Jarrow

Ellison St.

Western Rd.

Bus Stn.

Jarrow M

Willington Gut

Viaduct

Wallsend

Rolling Mill Rd.

Blackett St.

Tyne Approach

Wagonway Rd.

Hebburn

Hebburn M

Ellison Street

Lyon St.

Argyle St.

Prince Consort Road

Walk 3

1   2   3   4   5   6   7   8   9   10   11   12   13

4   5   6   7   8   9

P

M

the Bede's World heritage area so that you can decide whether to linger awhile or return for a longer visit another time. Opposite the Allison Arms turn right into Church Bank. Shortly after the River Don Bridge, steps and a side road, turn right into the **Monastery Grounds** to visit **St Paul's Church (6)** dedicated in 685 AD by Benedict Biscop (open daily 10.00am to 4.30pm). The original Chancel remains. Cross Church Lane and the grounds of the former Jarrow Hall, up steps to **Bede's World and Museum (7)**. Retrace your steps down the stone steps and path turning left at the picnic area, down more steps into Slake Road. Turn left (you may prefer the adjacent path between the road and the Don, skirting the pylons). The walk continues along the metalled cycle path (signed), which shortly branches off to the left, but it is worth continuing to the end of Slake Road (before returning to that path), for excellent river views **(8)**. You may well see to your right across the Don a car-carrying vessel beside the huge Nissan Quay on reclaimed Jarrow Slake. Follow the cycle path into Curlew Road until it emerges onto the main road (Priory Road), keep right and after about 100 yds turn right towards a Gasometer, with the 'Gaslight' pub ahead on your left. You will emerge onto the riverside at the attractive (though when I was there in 2004, suffering a bit of vandalism) **Riverside Park (9)**. Keep right to the Charles Palmer statue whose inscription encapsulates Jarrow's history. Steps lead down from the statue to the Riverside walk; turn left and continue to the **Pedestrian Tunnel (10)** entrance (turn left to reach it, before the cobbled road, which is a dead end). You might like to make the subterranean (sub fluvial?) crossing to the North bank of the river. The Tunnel is open 24 hours a day and free. Leaving the Tunnel entrance aim for the inverted cone-shaped Road Tunnel ventilation shaft and turn right when you come to the main road (Chaytor Street). Follow this road to the roundabout and, if you wish to omit the next stretch (to Hebburn) continue straight on along Ellison Street to Jarrow Bus and Metro Stations. Otherwise continue right into Western Road past the vast land reclamation and rebuilding of the former Jarrow Mill (in progress when this book was being compiled) bringing you sharply across the 15 centuries from Bede to the present day redevelopment of the Tyne. Turn right into **Rolling Mill Road (11)** as you enter Blackett Street but keep straight on where Rolling Mill Road forks away to the right and within almost 50 yards turn right again at Tyne Approach. Follow the road down to the river bank **(12)** for splendid views of the shipyards opposite and the impressive Metro viaduct over Wellington Gut. Nearer to hand note the Marine Police HQ. Retrace your steps turning right from Tyne Approach into Rolling Mill Road to rejoin Blackett Street, which at the next roundabout becomes Wagonway Road (keep straight on at the roundabout - ignore road on right to Waggonway Industrial Estate) and then Lyon Street. Seek inspiration from the spire of **St Andrews Church (13)** which heralds the approach to much more attractive walking! The names of the many pubs along this urban stretch evoke memories of the old industries (Rolling Mill for example). Although the church was sadly locked on our visit, there are benches outside, which provide a pleasant view over attractive new housing to the riverside. Long distance walkers should turn right down Ellison Street to join Walk 3. To complete Walk 2 turn left at the end of Lyon Street and along Prince Consort Road to Hebburn Metro Station. [For further walks in this area ask at Tourist Offices for River Don Walks 1 and 2 and Walks Round Jarrow].

Walk 3: Hebburn To Newcastle (Swing Bridge) (linear)
Hebburn to Bill Quay only (circular)

Attractive walking through the Riverside Park and along Keelmans Way paved cycle path, there is plenty to see especially across the river, much attractive new development, like St Peters Basin, but many reminders of the 'old' river-staiths, buoys, machinery –and the delightful Bill Quay Community Farm.

Distance: *Hebburn to Pelaw Metro - 3 miles (4½ km)* **Time:** *1¼ hours*

Hebburn to Newcastle - 6 miles (9 km) **Time:** *2½ hours*

Terrain: *Metalled paths or firm field paths. No stiles or muddy paths under normal conditions.*

Transport: *Metro from Newcastle Central Station (directions at end of walk) back to Hebburn or from Pelaw to Hebburn if only walking to Bill Quay.*

Car Parks: *At Hebburn (near Metro) and Quayside and as shown on the walk map.*

Refreshments: *A number of pubs 'en-route' and a vast choice in Newcastle.*

Start: *Hebburn Metro.*

Turn right into Prince Consort Road and at the roundabout turn right into Lyon Street and shortly left down Ellison Street past **St. Andrew's Church (1)**. Continue down to the river bank and turn left along the attractive path which veers left at a metal fence to bring you onto the end of a road. Ignore the cycle way signs to Newcastle/Gateshead, but go straight ahead onto a grassy path which ends at Prince Consort Road. Where the road turns right down to the car park go straight ahead along the metalled path, past the **Hebburn Riverside Nature Trail notice board (2)**. This pleasant path, high above the river, affords splendid views. After about a mile, the path heads downhill to the right, so follow it rather than the rougher track straight ahead. Emerging past the '**Cricketers Inn**' **(3)** turn left up Cromwell Road. Should you wish to use the Pelaw Metro Station (perhaps after visiting Bill Quay Farm) continue south into Station Road and turn right into Shields Road (A185). The station is about ¼ mile further on, up a road on your left. To contine this walk, just before Station Road turn right into Haining Wood Terrace to the **Bill Quay Community Farm (4)**. The path continues along the south side of the main farm building. A delightful mixture of model and real farm animals including some rare breeds, this rural oasis in the midst of urban Tyneside is well worth a pause to visit. The path, continuing past the farm forks right downhill towards the river, where it rejoins Keelman's Way, whose distinctive signposts are a guide for most of the rest of the way to the Millennium Bridge. For a moment though you are now back on the river bank so take care over the next couple of hundred yards as there are steep drops on your right. Where the path becomes a road as you approach the **Factory**

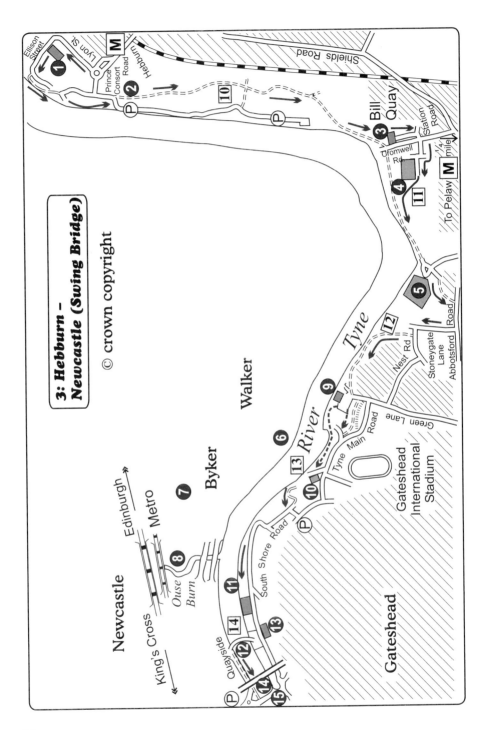

3: Hebburn –
Newcastle (Swing Bridge)

© crown copyright

Newcastle

Byker

Walker

Gateshead

Gateshead International Stadium

River Tyne

Edinburgh

Metro

King's Cross

Ouse Burn

Quayside

South Shore Road

Tyne Main Road

Green Lane

Abbotsford Road

Stoneygate Lane

Nest Rd

Ellison Street

Lyon St.

Prince Consort Road

Hebburn Road

Shields Road

Bill Quay

Station Road

Cromwell Rd.

To Pelaw

¼ mile

(5) fork left at the blue C2C sign but ignore the next one pointing left and continue straight ahead, crossing the road to rejoin the metalled path which leads round to the right with houses on your left and a high fence on your right with playing fields behind. Emerging into Abbotsford Road turn right again into Stoneygate

The Millennium Bridge

Lane and left, just past the factory car parks into Nest Road. Almost at once turn right down Keelmans Way and follow it above the river, whose steep banks on either side make it seem to be flowing through a gorge, to Green Lane, with the **Elephant (9)**, a possible refreshment stop on your right. Unfortunately the attractive riverside path is currently closed for the next ½ mile, so you must take the metalled path under the low hill just south of the Elephant, off Green Lane to the left, and follow this round to join the Tyne Main Road. Continue west along the road and down past the **"Schooner" (10)** to rejoin the path at the Car Park. Opposite is **St. Peter's basin (6)**, a housing/marina complex typical of much of the regeneration of the riverside with the allotments, pigeon sheds and old terraced housing on the hillside above providing memories of the past. Beyond the White Spillers Mill on the far bank is the unique and colourful **Byker Wall (7)** development and the **viaducts (8)** spanning the Ouse Burn. Look for Metro trains and HST 125's and 225s on their way to / from King's Cross and Edinburgh. From the Car Park a short stretch of path leads you up to South Shore Road. Follow this, but carry straight on after about ½ mile under the shadow of the **Baltic Arts Centre (11)**, past the **visitors' centre (13)** and down onto the **Millennium ('Blinking Eye') Bridge (12)**. Pause in midstream for a wonderful view of the Tyne Bridges (see Walk 4) of which it is, of course, the latest. Turn left along the Quayside past the impressive Law Courts and the floating night club "Tuxedo Princess" opposite, and under the **Tyne Bridge (14)** to reach the North end of the **Swing Bridge (15)**.

To get to Central Station and Newcastle City Centre either catch a bus from the Quayside or cross the road (take care, it is generally busy) at the end of the Swing Bridge and go up the long flight of steps (127 of them!) opposite to Castle Garth. Follow road signs to the Central – about 5 minutes' walk from the top of the steps.

Walk 4: Newcastle (Swing Bridge) to Scotswood Bridge (circular)

This follows the attractive Riverside Walk (and Keelman's Way on return). Much of the 19th century industry, which urbanised Elswick and Scotswood almost over-night has now given way to modern successors – Newcastle Business Park and the Gateshead Metro Centre. Long distance walkers are advised to do the outward (North bank) leg of this circular walk. The South bank return has one long (1½ miles) stretch of road, so, if it does not appeal, there are frequent return buses from Scotswood Bridge, which continue to/from Newburn so the outward halves of walks 4 & 5 could be combined for a 6 mile (10km) linear walk.

Turn west off the **Swing Bridge (1)**, down the steps (notice the Neptune sculpture on the old fish market), follow the attractively paved Riverside Walkway passing in front on the **Copthorne Hotel** and under the bridges for which Newcastle is justly famous.

[*Before the hotel is the* **High Level** *(road/rail)* **Bridge (2)** *(1841), then a series of three fine bridges spanning 80 years of engineering. Compare the impressive bulk of the* **King Edward VII** *(railway)* **Bridge (4)** *(1906) with the more slender lines of* **Queen Elizabeth II (3)** *(1978) and* **Redheugh (5) Bridges** *(1983) which carry, respectively, the metro and relief roads over the river. Plenty for bus and rail enthusiasts to spot passing overhead. Along the Riverside walkway there are information panels, courtesy of Northumbrian Water, describing the 19th century riverbank and its industries.*]

When you are roughly opposite the Federation Brewery across the river, with "The Home of Pils Lager" emblazoned along its roof, follow the metalled path up a to join William Armstrong Road before it briefly swings off left to come to steps leading up on your right back to the road again. Follow the road up to the traffic lights and turn left then continue along the pavement beside the fabled (in the Geordie's National Anthem 'Blaydon Races') Scotswood Road. Cross this road just after Whitehouse Road roundabout and follow the 'Hadrian's Way' sign up a wide metalled path on your right which then follows the line of the **North Wylam railway (6)** parallel to the road below [The route continues on map 5]. Continue along the old railway track until you come to the footbridge, over the A695, on your left just before the roundabout at the north end of **Scotswood Bridge (7)**. If continuing to Newburn now follow Walk 5. To return to Swing Bridge via the South bank cross the footbridge, turn right to the pavement and follow it round left over Scotswood Bridge, bearing left at the far side, before descending steps or ramp, crossing a strip of grass to the riverside road and turning right to the powerboat marina. The river here is tidal and at low tide the thick glutinous mud reveals much debris of former use, barge and jetty timbers for example. Pass either side of the Marina building and keep right to the railway pedestrian crossing. Stop! Look! Listen! And cross with care. Keep left past the **Skiff** and continue to the left of the "**Express by Holiday**

4: Newcastle (Swing Bridge) – Scotswood Bridge

Note: Please see Walk 5 for continuation West to Scotswood Bridge

© crown copyright

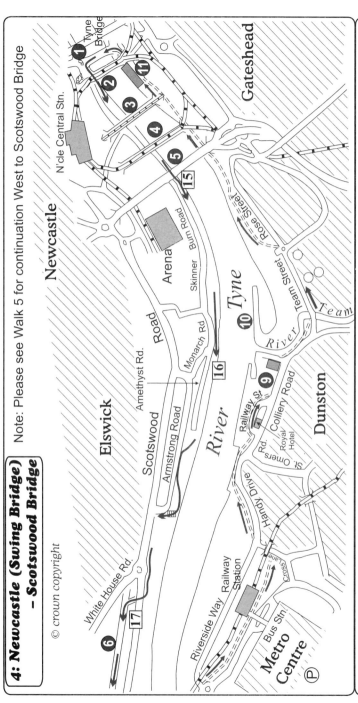

Distance: 6 miles (10 km) (Swing Bridge to Scotswood bridge 3 miles (5km)).

Time: 3/3½ hrs.

Terrain: Metalled paths/ pavements. Steps. No stiles.

Transport: Frequent buses from Scots-wood Bridge to Central Station and Newcastle City Centre; and every ten minutes from New-burn (number 21 &22).

Car parks: Quayside, Scotswood bridge – on road side (side streets), Newburn (see Walks 5&6 map), Metro centre.

Refreshments: Scotswood Bridge ('Skiff'), Metro Centre, several pubs on the return leg.

Start: North end of Swing Bridge.

17

Inn" (8) sign at the car park edge to join the path over the tubular arched foot-bridge beside the railway over the Derwent. The path continues under Riverside Road and along beside the railway and is surprisingly secluded, flanked by brambles and bulrushes in places, though disappointingly litter prone too. It regains road level beside the Metro Centre Station (not, confusingly, on the Tyne and Wear Metro) and you see the impressive frontages of the Centre and the mirrored Metroland. If you wish to call in at either, there is no pedestrian road crossing, so do take care, as the traffic is busy. Where the path meets Cross Lane turn left (signed) under the railway, cross Handy Drive turn right and continue beside Handy Drive, St. Omer's Road. Railway Street and Colliery Road, with frequent glimpses of the river on your left. It is also possible to make out the old tracks of the railway leading to the splendid **Dunston Coal Staiths (10)** just past the **Tudor Rose (9)**.

[*Renovated for the Gateshead Garden Festival of 1990, the Staiths were in use from 1893 to 1979 providing transhipment of coal from 38 local collieries to ocean going colliers. Sadly the festival site and staiths are no longer accessible, though this area is shortly to be redeveloped.*]

A few hundred yards after the Tudor Rose veer left into Team Street and where it joins Rose Street turn left down Keelman's Way – a metalled path, which takes a pleasant route beside the river with wonderful views of all the bridges, to join the road by the **Ovoline Factory (11)** leading to the Swing Bridge.

Walk 5: Scotswood Bridge to Newburn (circular)

The paths through the new Newburn Riverside development linear Park and Walbottle Brickworks Nature Reserve provide a much better round than my original Walk 5 which returned through Blaydon largely along streets. The blocking off of the short section through Scotswood railway tunnel, due to security problems is a disappointment but overall this is a much improved walk.

> **Distance**: *6 miles (10km) (Scotswood Bridge to Newburn 3 miles (5 km))*
> **Time**: *3/3 ½ hours*
> **Terrain**: metalled paths/pavements. Grass, Steps/ramps. No stiles
> **Transport**: *As for walk 4.*
> **Car Parks**: *Mainly on road (side streets), Newburn (see Walk 5/6 map), Blaydon.*
> **Refreshments**: *Pubs en route to Newburn.*
> **Start**: *North end of Scotswood Bridge (7) at North side of the A695 footbridge (1)*

Turn West from the footbridge along Hadrian's Way, but where the Way turns right keep straight on down to the A6085. Cross this road at the traffic lights, turn right

18

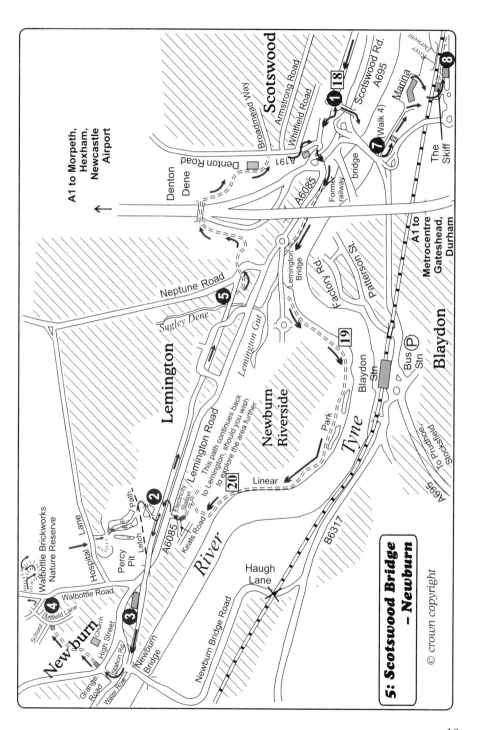

5: Scotswood Bridge – Newburn

© crown copyright

and shortly down to the riverside walkway which brings you to the new Lemington Bridge. Cross it and at the twin portals to Newburn Riverside turn left to the riverside path, following it for 1½ miles until it leaves the river. Turn left where it continues to the right, climb steps to Keats Road and turn right onto the A6085. Cross almost at once to the bus stop by the Percy Pit sign where an opening in the fence bring you onto the **railway trackbed (5)**. Turn left and follow the wide path over Skew Bridge, past (on your right) **Spencers Steel Works building (3)**, typical of a former heavy industry, which closed in 1926. To continue on Walk 6 cross the road keeping slightly left into Water Row.

To complete Walk 5 cross the road, turn right, then left into Station Road and, after a few yards, follow it as it bears right up the hill to the traffic lights on High Street. Cross the road, climb the 19 steps to the War Memorial and continue ahead, along the rising path which soon comes out into grassland with housing on right. Steps will take you down to Milfield Lane. You pass a school on your left and **Hareside Close** on your right **(4)** as you follow the Lane round right to join Walbottle Road. Turn left and almost at once cross the road and enter the old quarry at the Walbottle Brickworks Nature Reserve sign. The gravel path zig zags up the quarry face to the top where you keep right but then straight on, ignoring side turns, through grassland with lovely views westwards along the Tyne Valley. Turn left into Hospital Lane and cross it and a low fence into fields, just before housing. There is no path here (over the old Percy Pit spoil heaps) but, if you continue straight ahead, once over the top you will come to the path just to the right of the apex of a fenced plantation. Follow this downhill as it passes through a wide 'ride' with a second fenced plantation on your right. Emerging onto a wide open area cross a wide metalled path ("Letch Path") and you will see a wooden walkway over a pond under electric power lines. Cross the pond and a short path will take you back onto the **railway trackbed (2)**. Turn left and continue for a mile until the trackway becomes **Otteringam Close (5)** which you follow onto Neptune Road - keep ahead and slightly right to the cycleway crossing of Neptune Road. Cross and continue up the metalled path which swings round and up the hillside to the footbridge over the busy A1. Take the right hand fork on the far side and follow the signposted path round left then right to Denton Road. Continue on the pavement downhill, passing the wall above the old tunnel portal to a Pelican crossing. Cross, turn right, then left onto the short roadway, following the Hadrian Way signs, turn right at a metal security fence then left to retrace your steps to the footbridge.

Walk 6: Newburn to Wylam (circular)

Out in the country at last! Although within sight of the edge of the built up area this really is a country walk. Trees conceal all of Ryton, opposite, except the church spire and there is real silence - a tranquil stretch. Cormorants, herons and other birds frequent the River. You may wish to visit George Stephenson's Cottage as you approach Wylam. There are two choices of route to Wylam, the metalled cycle way, which follows the North Wylam Railway or the clearly defined, mainly sandy, sometimes muddy, path, which hugs the riverbank and affords close up views of the bird life.

Distance: 6 miles (10 km) - Newburn to Wylam 3¼ miles (5 km) **Time**: 3/3½ hrs

Terrain: Metalled paths or sandy/muddy riverside path (boots suggested) (Your choice). No stiles or steps (unless you wish to use them/ramp available). 3 kissing gates.

Car Parking: at Newburn and Wylam

Refreshments: Pubs at Newburn and Wylam. Restaurant at Wylam

Start: Newburn Bridge (north end)

For this circular walk 6 follow directions for the Newburn-Wylam riverbank path: to reach which cross the road at Newburn Bridge into Water Row. Pass the front of **Boathouse Inn (1)**, and continue along the metalled path under the electricity wires with a pylon to your right until you cross a footbridge and come to the Tyne Riverside Country Park Car Park where there is a useful map of the immediate area. Cross the Car Park and skirt the slip way at the head of which is the **Visitors Centre (2)**, for more local information (and toilets). Open in the summer months the Centre provides various booklets with local walks exploring the Industrial Heritage of the area. Return to the riverbank beyond the slipway and continue along the path with a play area on your right. This is well-defined and just before the signpost 'Wylam 2 miles', take the left fork "Hadrian's Wall Path" (with an acorn motif) and go through a kissing gate. The path needs care being narrow, muddy and with quite a steep drop down to the river in places. It is a pretty path with attractive views across the river to **Ryton Church** tower **(3)** peeping out over the trees and an array of flowers in season - look out for Lady's Slipper, Yarrow, Michaelmas Daisy - look out too for the **Tidestone (4)** of 1783, marking where the Tyne ceases to be tidal. Just after this the path makes a slight detour from the bank, before returning at a particularly steep section. Where Hadrian's Wall Path turns right follow it and turn left onto the Waggonway to avoid a difficult stretch of riverside path. Where Hadrian's Wall Path turns off to the right, you should turn left through a gate to regain the riverside path. After half a mile you enter the **Close House Riverside Reserve (5)** and traverse the edge of a Golf Course, emerging into a clearing with picnic tables.

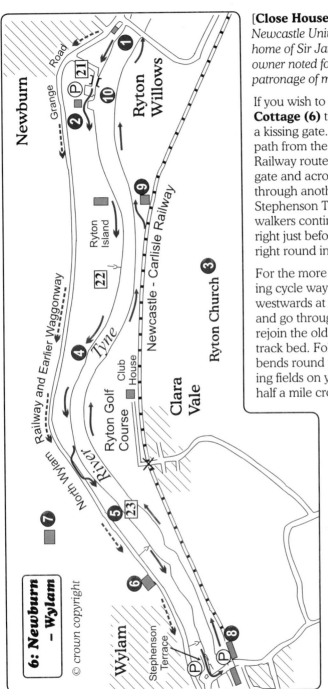

Newburn

Grange Road

Ryton Willows

Railway and Earlier Waggonway

Ryton Island

Newcastle – Carlisle Railway

Tyne

River

North Wylam

Ryton Golf Course

Club House

Ryton Church

Clara Vale

Wylam

Stephenson Terrace

6: Newburn – Wylam

© crown copyright

[**Close House (7)**, *now owned by Newcastle University, is the former home of Sir James Knott, a coal/ship owner noted for his philanthropy and patronage of many local trusts etc.*]

If you wish to visit **Stephenson's Cottage (6)** turn right through a kissing gate. To return to the path from the Cottage or from the Railway route go back through the gate and across the field; continue through another kissing gate into Stephenson Terrace. Long distance walkers continuing on Walk 7 turn right just before the bridge and keep right round into the car park.

For the more direct but less interesting cycle way route cross the road westwards at the Newburn Bridge and go through the open gateway to rejoin the old North Wylam railway track bed. Follow this path as it bends round to the left with playing fields on your left. After about half a mile cross Grange Road and continue along the old railway, which is now the cycle way, swapping sides again after another mile. The path passes **George Stephenson's Cottage (6)** 'High Street House' (National Trust, currently open 2 to 5pm. Weds, Thurs, Sats, Suns April to October). Continue on from the cottage to Wylam Car Park (site of the old North Wylam station). Long distance walkers would then continue on Walk 7.

To complete Walk 6 back to Newburn turn left out of Stephenson's Terrace to cross the river and turn left into **Wylam Station (8)** car park. The station, built in 1835, is one of the oldest still in regular use, in the world. At the end of the car park follow the Keelman's Way sign on to the path that squeezes between railway and river until it emerges onto the edge of Ryton Golf Course and continue to Newburn bridge. Watch out for low flying golf balls! Where the railway again comes near the river bank you pass **Ferry House (9)**, marking the southern end of the ferry crossing from Ryton Island, which in the early 19th century was an island, the river then being much wider and shallower. The ferryman lived on the island - until his house was washed away in a flood! As you pass through the gorse bushes of **Ryton Willows (10)**, where horses often graze, notice the timber remains of boats and barges dumped when no longer seaworthy. Steps or a ramp lead up to Newburn Bridge, cross it to complete the walk.

Walk 7: Wylam to Ovingham / Prudhoe (circular)

An attractive walk across the old North Wylam railway bridge (a mini Tyne Bridge in appearance), following the course of the river, and passing the Spetchells (an early example of reclamation of an industrial site. Spoil from the wartime ICI works has now been successfully grassed and treed to provide a line of low hills concealing the factories from the walker). The return path passes beside Prudhoe Castle and although it overlooks the industrial bypass area is largely sheltered by trees in summer and is particularly pretty approaching Hagg Bank.

> **Distance**: 5 miles (8 km), Wylam to Prudhoe 2½ miles (4 km)   **Time**: 2½ hrs
> **Terrain**: metalled roads/paths or firm paths - unless you use the rougher riverside paths in Wylam (with steps) and past the Spetchells (see text). Kissing Gate.
> **Transport**: Low Prudhoe to Prudhoe centre and Newcastle Arriva 604   half-hourly.
> **Car Parking**: Wylam, Prudhoe
> **Refreshments**: Wylam and Ovingham. Adam & Eve - Low Prudhoe.
> **Start**: Wylam car park

If you want to stick close to the river return to Wylam Bridge and go down steps on the left and under the bridge to join the rough sandy path, which will be submerged whenever the river rises by more than a couple of feet. Ignore a flight of steps ahead of you but continue alongside the river until steps take you up to the old **Railway Bridge (1)**. The easier route is to continue along the old track bed from the car park passing under the main road to reach the Railway Bridge. Continue across it and up the path beside the existing railway line to the junction in Hagg Bank. Turn right at the sign: 'Tyne Riverside Way to Low Prudhoe – 2 miles' and follow the road which soon crosses a cattle grid into open grassland. At a second cattle grid go through Hagg Farm and then follow the road beside the Spetchells to Ovingham Bridge. There are paths nearer the river if you wish to leave the road by the various stiles/gates on the right. Pass under the bridge and turn left into the **Riverside Country Park** car park **(2)** unless continuing on to Walk 8.

To return to Wylam turn right onto the road leading to Prudhoe Station, cross the level crossing, and proceed with care over the bypass (A695) to the left of the roundabout (where you will find the 604 Prudhoe – Newcastle bus stop) and up the steps (or round on the pavement) into Station Road, turning left into **Prudhoe Castle** approach road. You will see a 'Footpath' sign. The castle is well worth a visit. Immediately after the castle cross a stone bridge on a wide path, but then turn sharply left downhill on a narrower one (signposted Hagg Bank 1½). Follow this as it skirts the edge of the woods. After half a mile, this broadens into a bridleway (currently very muddy and rutted by construction vehicles). Follow it briefly round right to a new road (cross this south of a roundabout **(3)**. On the far pavement turn left (North) at a three-armed signpost "Hagg Bank ¾" and just before the path rises to join the road, turn right between a small plantation and the wooded hillside. Continue along the edge of the woods parallel to the bypass with a field on your left. The path turns left to a gate, after which you must cross the bypass. Follow the 'Footpath' sign opposite through another gate into a small planta-

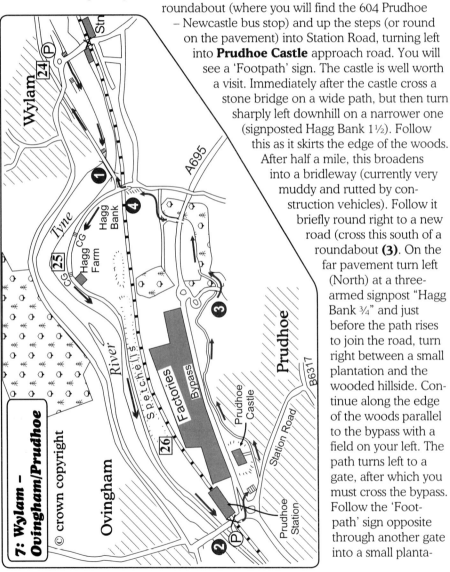

Prudhoe Castle

tion where a road goes off left, keep right but shortly look out for the way mark indicating left. Follow this path through a narrow valley **(4)** before keeping right uphill through a kissing gate onto a road. Turn left, cross the railway bridge into Hagg Bank and turn right to re-cross the old railway bridge and return to Wylam.

Walk 8: Prudhoe to Stocksfield (circular)

A pretty walk, mainly on good paths through fields, but there are stiles to climb; we are really out into the country now with distant views of Hexhamshire. Start and finish can be in the pretty village of Ovingham. En route, short diversions take you to Thomas Bewick's home of Cherryburn and the delightful twin churches and castle at Bywell.

Distance: 7½ miles (12 km). Prudhoe to Stocksfield 3 miles (5 km).
Time: 3½ hours (plus any time at Cherryburn or Bywell).
Terrain: Short stretches of road, mainly firm field or woodland paths or grass. 20 stiles + 2 kissing gates.
Car parking: Low Prudhoe, Stocksfield station.
Refreshments: Ovingham and Ovington, Adam & Eve, Low Prudhoe
Start: Prudhoe Riverside Country Park car park, or in Ovingham, in which case cross the bridge over the Tyne and turn right into the car park.

Turn left onto the riverside path **(1)** and follow this to the railway foot crossing. Cross with care and follow the steep, sometimes muddy bridleway up veering right between high banks to emerge from the woods at the **Hammerite Paint Factory (2)**. At the A695 turn right, follow it for a few yards then turn right down the road which leads to the Factory Car Park. Almost immediately turn left along the rough road to the metalled road at **Eltringham House (3)**. Turn left, bear right, past old works buildings, but where the road veers sharp left continue straight on following direction of signpost 'Merryshields 1¼' [You may wish to continue 100 yards or so up the metalled road to visit **Cherryburn (4)**, home of the engraver, Thomas Bewick (National Trust)]. Continuing the walk follow the tractor wheel marks straight across the field to a gateway **(5)**, turn right down a farm road and immedi-

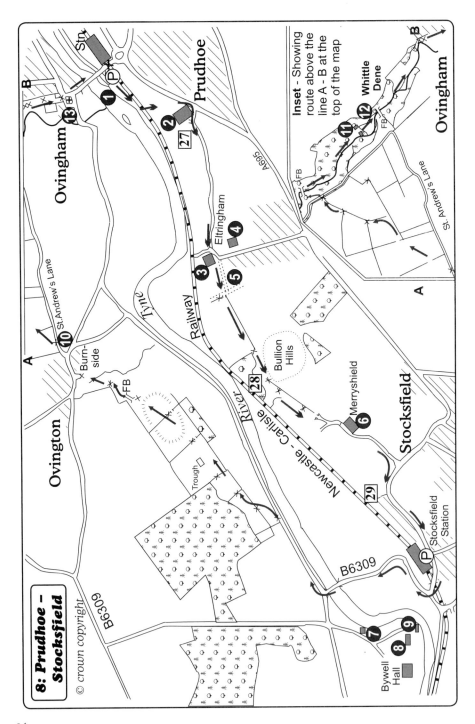

8: Prudhoe – Stocksfield

© crown copyright

Inset - Showing route above the line A - B at the top of the map

Whittle Dene

Ovingham

Prudhoe

Ovingham

Ovington

Stn

St. Andrew's Lane

St. Andrew's Lane

A695

Eltringham

Tyne

Railway

River

Newcastle - Carlisle

Bullion Hills

Merryshield

Stocksfield

Stocksfield Station

B6309

B6309

Bywell Hall

Burn-side

FB

Trough

27

28

29

1 2 3 4 5 6 7 8 9 10 11 12 13

26

ately left over a second stile into a field with a fence on the left, which you should follow to climb another stile in the top left-hand corner. Keep right round the slope of Bullion Hills passing well to the left of a silver birch copse and downhill to reach a stile over a wire fence protecting the wood which now covers old mine spoil heaps. Keep along to the right of this fence. Cross two more stiles and through a metal gate where the path becomes a (sometimes) muddy grass bridleway which joins a farm road bending left then right to pass through a gate in front of **Merryshields Farm (6)**. Continue along the farm road, which brings you to the A695. Turn right and follow this round past Stocksfield Station and over the railway, at which point long-distance walkers would continue on Walk 9.

Turn right onto the B6309 (to 'Bywell and Stamfordham') and continue along the road, crossing the Tyne bridge. To visit **Bywell** with its **castle (7)** and twin churches of **St. Andrew (8)** and **St. Peter (9)**, turn left at the of the bridge, and follow the footpath ('Bywell ½ mile'). To continue the walk turn right along the riverside road. After less than half a mile cross the ladder stile on your left, signposted 'Ovington 1 mile'. The route bears diagonally right through two fields joined by another ladder stile. After that just follow the waymarks on each stile gradually uphill across the next two fields, until you come out onto a grassy ridge in the third. Go diagonally left down to the stile and footbridge in the far left corner. Turn left, follow the field edge to the next stile and climb up the steep hill, diagonally right this time as Ovington comes into view, to a stone stile by a gate leading into Burnside. At the main road turn right and when it veers right just past the Winships shop and restaurant, go straight on to the left of the **Ovington Social Club (10)** into St. Andrews Lane. Ignore the first path to Overdene, but shortly after climb the stile at signpost 'Whittle Dene ¾'. Follow this clear pathway through fields (see inset to main map). After the second gap descend to the slight dip and turn left following the field edge. Cross three waymarked stiles into woodland. Cross the footpath that follows the top edge of the woods taking the middle path bearing left downhill. Whittle Dene appears far below to the right. At the bottom is a Woodland Trust information board after which you cross the bridge and turn right taking the right fork 200 yards later. After some pleasant walking along the Dene you reach a couple of ruined buildings **(11)** on either side of the path and shortly afterwards the quaint wooden bungalows, which reminded me of a settlement in the Appalachian Hills of Virginia **(12)**. Continue along a clear path, out of the woods through a kissing gate and cross a field to another kissing gate where you can see the path going up a short hill towards houses. At the top cross 2 stiles and follow the path, with housing on the left and a steep drop on the right, to another stile. Cross this, pass a bungalow, and onto a short track with a metal gate ahead. Cross the stone stile beside it. Turn left along the road past the **church (13)** (where Thomas Bewick is buried), turn right, and then left downhill to Ovingham Bridge and back to the start.

Walk 9: Stocksfield to Riding Mill (linear or circular)

There is no right of way beside the river so we move inland through pretty woodland up to the hamlet of Broomley. Open stretches afford fine views of the Tyne Valley and beyond. To make this a circular walk return via the A695. This is an attractive road though quite busy. There is a tarmac footpath on the right hand side as far as the layby just beyond Low Shilford, continuing shortly thereafter on the other side of the road. The bus is perhaps a more attractive option (see Introduction)!

Distance: 3 miles (5km)   **Time**: 1½ hours

Terrain: Woodland paths, fields, sometimes muddy. Short stretch of road. 7 (or 8) stiles, 2 (or 4) kissing gates.

Car parking: Stocksfield and Riding Mill stations – small car park beside B6309 (see map)

Refreshments: 'Wellington' Inn – Riding Mill

Start: Stocksfield Station.

Turn right onto A695. Follow the road over railway towards Riding Mill. Turn left into B6309 ('Ebchester'). Re-cross the railway and turn right into small car park **(1)**. Leave it through a small gap on the left (beyond which is an information map of the area), turn right and join the clear path leading over the grass. Keep straight on where another waymarked path leads off left, but at the next fork in this wide path turn left towards a line of tall pines **(2)** on the skyline. When you reach these another broad path forms a 'T – junction'. Turn right and at another 'junction' turn left signposted 'Broomley ½' and follow the waymarks skirting mature woodland into which you turn right, just before a field fence. The path continues left along the edge of the wood with a steep bank on your right sloping down to Smithy Burn which you cross by a tiny stone bridge **(3)** after the path emerges from the trees via a stile. Keep left and continue across the field to a stile and gate leading to a farm road. Turn right and proceed over the crossroads into Broomley continuing along the road for about half a mile (ignore junction to left) until you come to a stile signposted 'Public Footpath' on your right. The path follows a hedge crossing a stile and the farm road, which leads to Roe House. Continue over a stile by a gate to Shilford West Wood, turn left along its edge to an opening beside a square pillbox type building **(4)**. The path goes through this opening and veers left then right down the edge of the wood before forking left into the wood. After a couple of hundred yards look out for a waymark directing you right to cross a broad ride (waymarked). The path takes you down through a broad area of blackberries to a stile leading out of the woods into a field. A kissing gate and steps take you down to the A68. Cross this with great care and go down further steps to another kissing gate, where waymarks offer you a choice of locally numbered paths. Railway enthusiasts may prefer number 2, which takes you past **Wentworth Grange (5)** through kissing gates

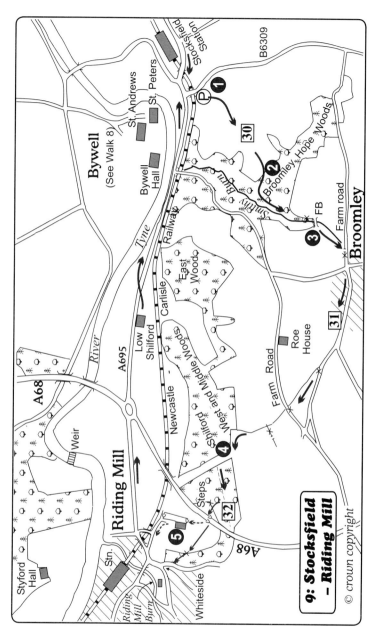

providing access to a fenced-off pathway. Turn left and follow a lane beside the railway to join the A695. Long-distance walkers turn left into Whiteside to continue on Walk 10. Alternatively follow path 3 from the A68 crossing straight ahead on a clearly defined path to a stile. The path continues down through woodland to the road (Whiteside). Turn right to the A695.

Walk 10: Riding Mill to Corbridge (linear or circular)

At the time of writing, flood erosion at Farnley Scar has made the riverside path impassable, so the Prospect Hill route, equally attractive, with wide-ranging views, must be followed at present. However, there are plans to realign the riverside path with a short inland diversion at the scar. New signposts at Riding Mill and Corbridge will show when the route is open. You will then have a choice of either route (for long-distance walkers), or the circular walk on its own. For both routes the outward direction will be East to West, with a note in the middle for those returning via the riverbank to Riding Mill.

Distance: 7½ miles (12½ km). Riding Mill to Corbridge via Prospect Hill – 4 miles (6½km); via riverbank 3½ miles (5½ km).

Time: 3½ hours.

Terrain: Road, paths, fields (Prospect Hill). Steps, one short steep section on each route, 5 stiles.1 kissing gate (riverside).

Car parking: Riding Mill station, Corbridge Bridge End.

Refreshments: Wellington Inn, Riding Mill (5), Ramblers Country House Restaurant (1), Valley Indian Restaurant (2), Dyvels Inn at Corbridge station (3). Large choice in Corbridge.

Start: Junction A 695 / Whiteside Bank

Prospect Hill Route

Walk up Whiteside Bank, turn right into Church Lane and right again onto the path beside St. James Church, cross the Riding Mill (or March) Burn and immediately take the path to the left and steps up to Millfield Road. Turn left, follow the road over the Burn and soon right into Marchburn Lane. After crossing the Burn (yet again) follow the Lane sharp left and look out for a narrow path just before a 'Private Road' sign. Follow this up between 'Treetops' and 'Marchburn', turn right into Sandy Lane and follow the road round to the left, then go right down the Private Road next to the house 'Beech Tree Corner' (to your right) to junction of A695 and a minor road. Turn left up the latter, keeping left at the next junction and shortly passing a large house 'Beauclerc' on your left. Almost at once you will see a signpost by a gate to 'Riding Hills' on your right beside Lea Grange. Follow the path to Riding Hills, following waymarks over a stile through a gate and round left past the farm to a road. Turn left and then take the next road on the right up to the top of Prospect Hill. At the crossroads turn right ('Corbridge 1½ miles'). Where the road turns left at Prospect Hill Farm go straight ahead over a stone stile and down beside and then through woods – a muddy path littered with tree debris – to cross a road, and over another stone stile into fields. Keep straight on over a ladder stile to a final stone stile in the wall beyond leading to the road. Turn right, follow this to the A695,

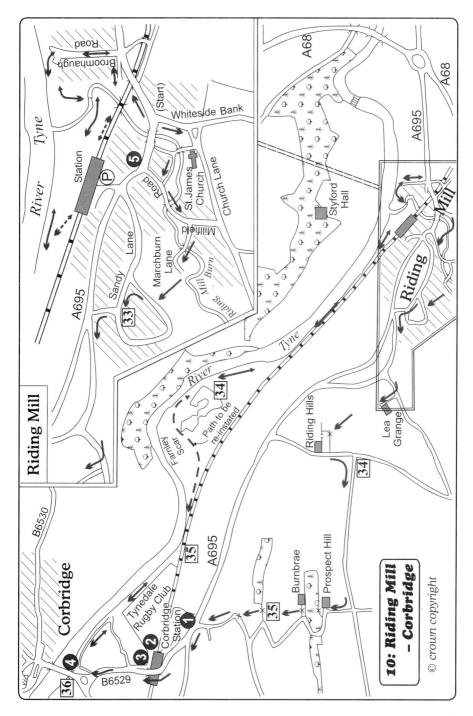

10: Riding Mill – Corbridge

© crown copyright

31

turn left and follow the B6529 down past the **'Ramblers' (1)**, **Corbridge Station (Valley Restaurant) (2), 'Dyvels' (Inn) (3)** to the **Bridge End (4)**.

[*Corbridge is a very pretty village, which deserves exploring. St. Andrews Church dates back to Saxon times. Corstopitum Roman Fort and museum is half a mile out of the village. Aydon Castle, a recently restored medieval fortified farm house is well worth a visit either by car or a pleasant 2 mile walk through fields and woods. Further afield are Slaley Hall – International Golf Course, Hotel and Conference Centre (4 miles SW) and the delightful village of Blanchland some 6 miles further on.*]

Corbridge

To return to Riding Mill, once the path is reinstated, take the unmade-up road leading East from the Bridge End, which turns into a path between Tynedale Rugby Club grounds and the river. Keep on until you reach a waymarked route over the disused railway tunnel and down past gravel pits to rejoin the clear path along the riverbank to Riding Mill, following reverse of the Riverbank route (below)

The Riverbank route (not yet available throughout - see above)

From Riding Mill cross the railway on the A695 (heading East) and either turn immediately left down a metalled road between houses, leading to a path which takes you onto the station platform at the far end of which you join the riverside path through a kissing gate or, more interestingly – but not when the Burn is high – go down to the end of Broomhaugh Road and straight ahead to the river bank. Follow the path round left and across the Burn on low stepping-stones. Keep right where the path forks and you are now on the riverside path, which you follow to Corbridge looking out for the short diversion inland at the gravel pits.

Walk 11: Corbridge to Hexham (Linear)

A very pretty walk along the banks of the Tyne and Devil's Water and then up into extensive woodland – you may catch sight of deer – before emerging at Hexham Fellside for a panoramic view of the town - 'The Capital of Tynedale'.

Distance: 4½ miles (7 km)
Time: 2 hours
Terrain: Short stretch of road, paths/fields, a few rough, muddy stoney stretches, gates, 1 kissing gate, steps but no stiles
Refreshments: wide choice in both Corbridge and Hexham.
Car parking: Corbridge Bridge End, Hexham - Wentworth car park
Start: Corbridge Bridge End

Go through the metal kissing gate on the West side of the road by the traffic lights and either walk along the flood embankment or follow the path along the river bank. Look back at the lovely lines of the bridge built in 1674 and the only one to survive the great Tyne flood of 1771. After half a mile just opposite Corbridge Mill you can see, at low water, remains of the piers of the Roman bridge carrying Dere Street or Stanegate to Corstopitum. Continue, after emerging from gorse bushes gradually left to join the Devil's Water bank. Climb up steps to gates to cross the railway line (take care), follow the now narrow path to Dilston Farm up stone steps onto the A695 and right, over the bridge. At the far side of the bridge cross the road and turn left to follow the signpost 'Duke's House 1½, Hexham 3' onto the unmade road beside the Devil's Water. The road becomes a grassy lane after veering right at Dilston Mill. Dilston Castle ruins are visible to your left as you continue up the lane, round a gate, passing to the left of a cottage, through another gate (following 'footpath' direction sign) and gradually uphill to cross a farm road at Dilston Park Farm. You have good views of the Tyne Valley and Beaufront Castle. The path narrows following a former sunken road and enters Park Wood. Going here is a bit rough and can be wet, but, at a junction of tracks becomes a firm wide bridleway. Continue straight ahead past Duke's House (a former shooting lodge) – count the chimneys! Shortly after this you reach a broad field on your right. Turn right down the broad stone-based path at the field's West side. Follow this down a steepish stony slope, at the bottom of which it veers left, and becomes a grassy path to emerge from the woods at Fellside road. Follow this to join the main road. Turn right downhill keeping right at the next road junction to reach the T-junction of Eastgate with Battle Hill. Turn right here for Hexham Bus Station, but cross the Pelican crossing to your left and continue straight ahead down St. Mary's Chare or Back Street under an archway (notice traces of the old St. Mary's Church on the right hand wall leading to the arch) to enter the Market Place. For the plan of Hexham see Walk 12.

Hexham

[Hexham is well worth exploring. This ancient market town, though probably not a Roman centre (argument still rages on this point among historians) has a long history. The 12th / 13th Century Abbey covers the site of St. Wilfred's Church built in 674 AD of which the crypt remains and is a 'must' for visitors. Ripon Cathedral contains the only other Saxon crypt in Britain. Traces of the extensive medieval priory remain in and around the Abbey. The Market Place is host to many stall-holders on Tuesdays, the main market day. The Cattle Mart, one of the busiest in the North is now housed in modern buildings (1996) near the river. Opposite the Abbey across the Market Place are the Moot Hall and Old Gaol, which now houses the excellent Border History Museum.]

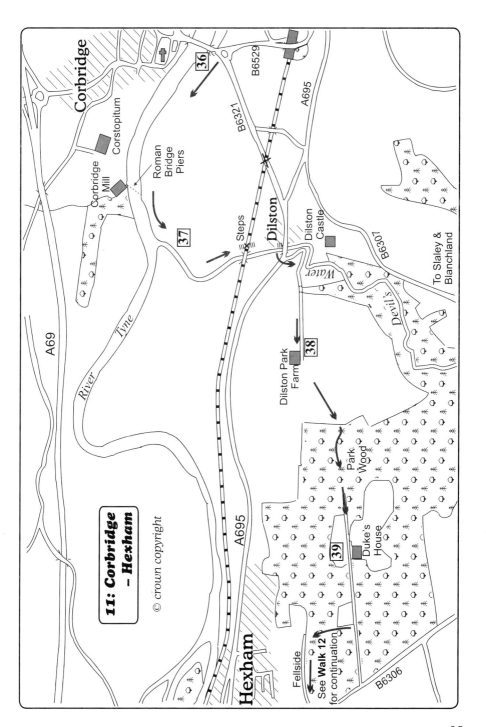

11: Corbridge – Hexham

© crown copyright

Corbridge

Corstopitum

Corbridge Mill

Roman Bridge Piers

A69

River Tyne

B6321

B6529

A695

Steps

Dilston

Dilston Castle

Water

Devil's

B6307

To Slaley & Blanchland

Dilston Park Farm

Park Wood

Duke's House

A695

Hexham

Fellside

See **Walk 12** for continuation

B6306

36

37

38

39

35

Hexham to Haydon Bridge

Walk 12: Hexham to Warden & Fourstones (circular)

Walk 13: Fourstones to Newbrough & Haydon Bridge (linear)

Long distance walkers are recommended to combine walks 12 and 13, not least because of public transport links at Hexham and Haydon Bridge. Buses to Newbrough and Fourstones are less frequent (see Introduction). Walk 12 could be split into two sections; Hexham to Warden and Warden to Fourstones (both circular). Long stretches of pretty riverbank as far as Newbrough, after which the route over Haydon Fell gives splendid views and a foretaste of the wide open spaces of the North Pennine Moors.

> **Distance**: Hexham to Haydon Bridge 10 miles (16 km), Hexham to Fourstones (circular) 9 miles (14½ km), the shorter Warden walks approx 4½ miles (7km) each.
>
> **Time**: Walk 12 - 4½ to 5 hours, Walk 13 - 4½ hours.
>
> **Terrain**: Mostly firm paths, short road stretches, and a few fields. Some narrow, rocky, uneven riverside sections. Steps, 1 stile.
>
> **Car parking**: Hexham – (Wentworth Car Park), elsewhere street parking.
>
> **Refreshments**: Wide choice in Hexham, 'Boatside' Inn – Warden, Fourstones – 'Railway' Inn, Newbrough – 'Red Lion', Haydon Bridge – several pubs.
>
> **Start**: Hexham Market Place.

Walk 12: Hexham to Warden & Fourstones (circular)

Go past the Forum Cinema, down Hallstile Bank and right at the roundabout. Cross the road (Pelican crossing) and continue ahead over the railway to the next roundabout turn left towards Tyne Green leaving the road almost at once to go past a café to the river bank. Turn left and follow the well-defined path with, on your left, Tyne Green Golf Course. At the end of which the path joins a metalled lane with the railway on your left. Shortly after passing the remains of piers of the old North Tyne Railway Bridge in the river, look out for a red waymark on a log indicating the Riverside Trail. Follow this down steps and round left to a footbridge over a rivulet and through rough gorse bushes to the riverbank. Go under the A69 bridge and climb up the flood embankment, along which the path continues. If high water covers the ground under the bridge, turn around and go through metal gates to rejoin the lane. Go under the A69 and at once turn right through a gate onto a path, which takes you back to the flood embankment. After passing Waters Meet (confluence of the North and South Tynes) and going under the railway bridge, the path emerges, between houses onto a road. For the shorter round turn left here, and follow instructions below.

For the Fourstones walk, turn right then right again at the main road. Cross the bridge to the 'Boatside' Inn. Continue left along the main road crossing over, just

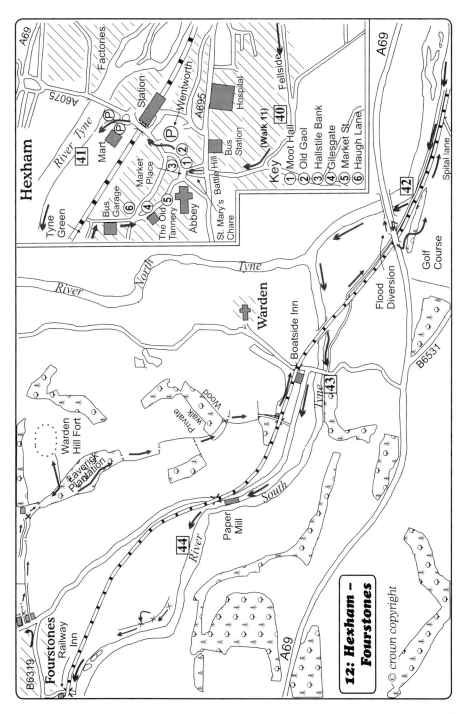

Hexham

A69

Factories

A6075

River Tyne

Tyne Green

Station

Wentworth

P P

P

Mart

Bus Garage

Market Place

③

① ②

⑥ ④ ⑤

The Old Tannery

St. Mary's Battle Hill Chare

Abbey

A695

Hospital

Bus Station

(Walk 11)

Key
① Moot Hall
② Old Gaol
③ Hallstile Bank
④ Gilesgate
⑤ Market St.
⑥ Haugh Lane

Fellside

40

41

North Tyne

River

Tyne

Warden

Boatside Inn

42

Flood Diversion

Golf Course

B6531

Spital Lane

A69

Warden Hill Fort

Laverick Plantation

Private walk

Wood

43

South

Tyne

River

Paper Mill

44

A69

Fourstones

Railway Inn

B6319

© crown copyright

12: Hexham – Fourstones

37

before the Level Crossing, to the Paper Mill and turn left at the signpost 'Fourstones 1½ Allerwash 2½'. Continue along the riverside path to Fourstones, crossing three stiles, the latter two to bypass path erosion. Long distance walkers continue straight ahead to join Walk 13. For Walk 12 turn right in front of a cottage, over level crossing gates and up the hill past The Railway Inn. Turn right at the main road, and then, after about ¼ mile, left where the main road curves to the right. Continue a short distance up this road and just before the last cottage on the right at a signpost ('Warden 2 Bridge End 2'). Climb over a stone stile beside a gate and almost at once at another signpost go right through a gate and slightly left across an open field to a post with a way mark on the back. Turn left onto a farm road and, shortly, through a metal gate. Follow a ride uphill, but look out for a way marked metal gate on your left, with a 3-armed signpost beyond it. Go through this and right up a road to a stile at Lavender Cottage. Follow the wall on your right to enter Laverick Plantation. If you want to visit Warden Hill Fort site for good views up the North Tyne take the next path on the left to a gate into a field and follow the wall on your right round and uphill to the Fort. Return the same way. Continue to a gate at the end of the trees. Continue along a field with a hedge on your right through a gate with the hedge now on your left to another gate. Continue slightly left to where a walled lane enters the field. Go down beside Private Walk Road and over a stone stile beside a gate. Just after this turn right through a wicket gate down the edge of a steep field to another gate in a wooden fence on the edge of wood. Continue down a sunken path to a couple of houses by a level crossing. Turn left as indicated by a waymark, and a signpost "Public Footpath, Bridge End" just before the left hand house and follow the path beside the railway to emerge onto a road. Turn right under the railway bridge, go straight ahead across the river and turn left into a metalled lane. Follow this, passing under the railway and A69. Immediately after the A69 bridge go left through a gate up steps across the bridge (there is a pavement) down steps beside the railway through a gate into woods. Follow the path over the old Allendale railway track up to the golf course. Turn left. Watch out for flying golf balls and skirt the edge of the course, climb some steps, join a path above a field to emerge into Spital Lane. Turn left to reach the road leading to Tyne Green. Follow this to a T-junction turn right past the bus garage, then across Haugh Lane and slightly left (notice The Old Tannery on your right – this area was the centre of Hexham's tanning industry some 2 centuries ago), up Gilesgate and Market Street to the Market Place.

Walk 13: Fourstones to Newbrough & Haydon Bridge (linear)

Distance: 5½ miles (9 km)
Start: Fourstones Railway Inn.

Cross the level crossing, and at the river bank turn right along the path, which is initially good, but erosion had made it quite difficult going as you approach Newbrough Burn though the final section has been repaired. [If the river is high follow the diversion shown on the map]. At the burn turn right under the railway bridge and right again up stone steps to a lane leading to B6319. Turn left then right again at signpost 'Newbrough ½', and follow a clear path through woods. Keep right at the ruined weir and left over a wooden bridge then straight on ignoring a fork to the right to come out, over a stone stile by a gate, turning left onto the Roman Stanegate linking Corstopitum with Vindolanda and Hadrian's Wall (turn right for the Red Lion). You might wish to visit St. Peter's Church. Built in 1865, this is the latest of a series of churches/chapels dating from the 12th century, dedicated to St. Peter (the 'Rock') perhaps because of the adjacent Stane ('stone') Gate, up which you continue for half a mile and turn left onto an unmade-up

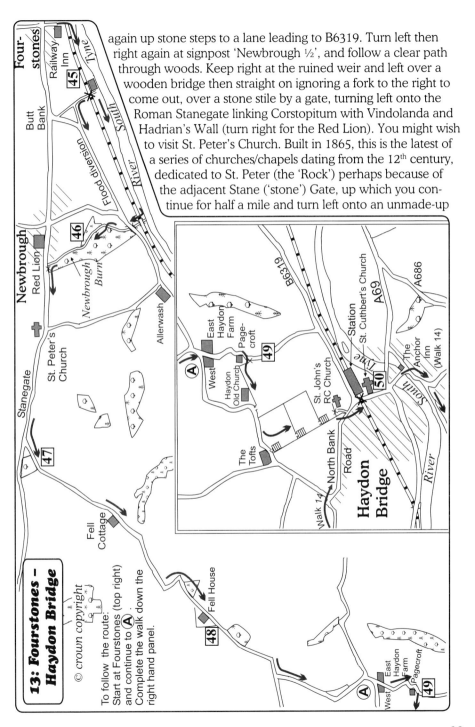

13: Fourstones – Haydon Bridge

© crown copyright

To follow the route. Start at Fourstones (top right) and continue to Ⓐ. Complete the walk down the right hand panel.

Fourstones
Railway Inn
Tyne
45
Butt Bank
River South
Flood diversion
46
Newbrough
Red Lion
Newbrough Burn
Allerwash
Stanegate
St. Peter's Church
47
Fell Cottage
Fell House
48

B6319
East Haydon Farm
Pagecroft
49
West Haydon Old Church
The Tofts
St. John's RC Church
North Bank
Walk 14
Road
Station
St. Cuthbert's Church
A69
Tyne
50
Tyne South
The Anchor Inn (Walk 14)
A686
River
Haydon Bridge
Ⓐ

Ⓐ
West
East Haydon Farm
Pagecroft
49

39

road by a small copse. No signpost at the time of writing. Continue along this firm walking for 1¾ miles until you reach a metalled road. Turn left down the road to East/West Haydon Farms. Keep left down the road between the two to Pagecroft, with its unusual garden 'furniture'. At the front of the house where the road turns left carry straight on (signpost 'Haydon Old Church ¼'), step across a rivulet, proceed over a stile across a field keeping diagonally right uphill towards the end of a tree-lined bank, follow this sharp right to a gate. The Old Church may be shut, but the Churchyard is worth a look. Turn left and down the road. Opposite the Tofts, go through the kissing gate ('Haydon Bridge ½') and down a steep field through 2 more gates (all with steps) and a stile to emerge past St. John's Church onto North Bank Road. Continue down to the A69, which can be crossed by the underpass to your left. Cross the old bridge to complete the walk at the Anchor Inn.

Haydon Bridge to Haltwhistle (3 circular or 1 linear)

Walk 14: Haydon Bridge to Allenbanks
Walk 15: Allen Banks to Willimoteswick & Shankfoot
Walk 16: Haltwhistle to Plenmeller & Warren House

Long distance walkers are recommended to combine Walks 14,15 and 16 following the outward legs of 14 and 15 then covering the pleasant country road from Shankfoot and Plenmeller, preferably continuing to Haltwhistle via the attractive Warren House section of Walk 16 or using the shorter routes suggested in the text. It is possible, also, to join or leave Walk 15 at Bardon Mill and/or divide it into two shorter circular walks - Allenbanks to Willimoteswick and Willimoteswick to Allenbank/Shankfoot. These are three varied and very beautiful walks, taking you up into higher ground, then down to the beautiful Allen Banks gorge, and back up to moorland. The Tyne is almost always in sight but lacks riverside paths in this area.

Distances: *Haydon Bridge to Haltwhistle 12½ miles (20 km) – could be shortened to 11 miles (17½ km)*

Haydon Bridge to Allen Banks (circular) – 7½ miles (12 km)

Allen Banks to Shankfoot (circular) – 7½ miles (12 km) – the shorter round to Willimoteswick would be 5 miles (8km)

Shankfoot to Plenmeller (the linear link for long distance walkers) 2 miles (road) (45 minutes)

Haltwhistle to Warren House (circular) 4 miles (6½ km)

Time / Terrain: *see each walk*

Car parking: *Allen Banks, Haydon Bridge and Haltwhistle (street parking)*

Refreshments: *pubs/cafés in Haltwhistle, pubs in Haydon Bridge.*

Walk 14: Haydon Bridge to Allen Banks (return via Whinnetley)

> **Terrain**: *Some roads, mainly fields, firm paths, steep descent at Allen Banks. Steps, 7 stiles*
>
> **Time**: *3½ hours*
>
> **Start**: *Haydon Bridge – Anchor Inn*

Turn West along the road and just after it bears left turn right down Lands End Road. Follow this pleasant road past the Willows Caravan site until after ¾ mile it veers sharp left. Go straight on (signpost 'Lees ½ Allen Banks 1½') to Lees Farm. With the farmhouse on your left go through two gateways into the farmyard. Turn left, with cottages on your right to a gate ('Allen Banks 1 mile'). Go through the gate, and turn right across a rivulet. Continue diagonally left up a steep slope, passing the left end of gorse bushes, punctuated by an equally steep dip, to a ladder stile over a wall. Continue across a field and through a gate to follow the wall line on your left before crossing another rivulet and veer slightly right to reach a stile in the wall ahead. Continue over the stile and down a wide track to another stile by a gate onto Tedcastle Farm road. Go left up this steep road and turn right at the T-junction. Go down hill for 200metres looking out for the 'Allen Banks' National Trust sign on a gate to your left (just after a right hand bend). Go through the kissing gate and follow the field track slightly left passing a clump of trees on your right. (*When logging takes place in exceptionally wet weather this track becomes so muddy and rutted that the paths are closed. In that case continue down the road to reach Allenbanks car park*). Ignore a gate further to your left, but continue to a kissing gate where you enter Allen Banks Nature Reserve. A wide path leads past Morralee Tarn and where steps come up from the tarn, turn right then left at a purple (currently) waymark (if it is pointing to the right as it was when I checked recently ignore it and continue left!) and follow the steep route of path and steps down to the River Allen suspension bridge – see more detailed map on page 43.

[*There is a delightful walk up to Plankey Mill, with excellent places for children to play en route if you have time. Take care where steep drops to the river border the paths. Once across the bridge turn left; follow the riverside path for 1½ miles to cross a second suspension bridge to the Mill where you can buy soft drinks and ices in summer. You can return on either side of the river*].

Cross the bridge, turn right along the riverside path. Long distance walkers should look out for steep flight of steps on the left, which you climb to join Walk 15. Walk 14 continues through Allen Banks car park (toilets available) to a road. Turn left and follow this turning right under the railway at Ridley Hall gates to cross the river and join the A69. Go a short way along the verge on your right to Bowershield. Cross the road with care to the lay-by opposite. Note the otherwise excellent OS Map is slightly wrong here, as it places Whitechapel Farm directly on the A69 and ignores

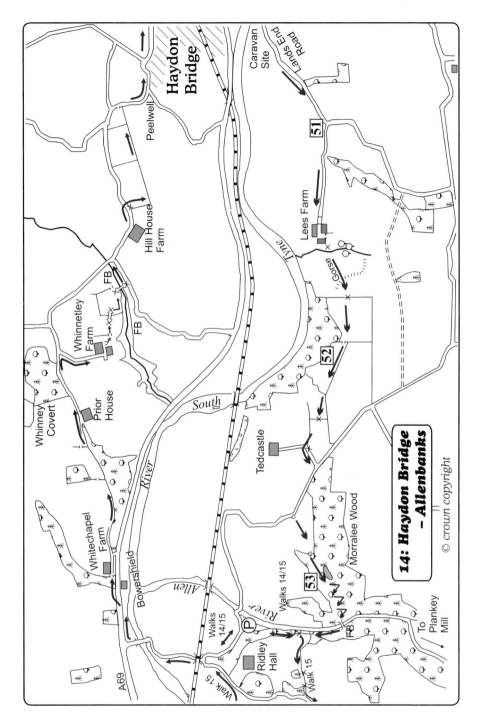

14: Haydon Bridge – Allenbanks

© crown copyright

the farm's approach road. Follow the wide grassy track beside the road from the lay-by. Ignore the footpath sign pointing left to High Meadow and Whitshields and continue up a slope to a small metal gate. Pass in front of Whitechapel Farm on the metalled approach road and continue ahead and slightly left on a roughly metalled farm road branching off the approach road where the latter drops down to the A69. Where this farm road ceases to be stone-based and turns sharp left at a metal gate, go ahead through this gate and over a field, beside a wood, to another metal gate, leading to a muddy bridleway through woods to join a road at Prior House. Continue past Whinney Covert and take the road (right) to Whinnetley Farm. Go past some buildings and turn left (where the farm road goes right) past the Farm House to a gate on your right with a yellow waymark. Go through this and a second gate, and keep diagonally left across a field to double stiles separated by a footbridge. Turn right down the side of this field and follow the fence left to a gate, just before which cross a stile on your right, over a footbridge and diagonally left across a field to a stile by a footpath sign. Ignore the sign opposite as the pathway in the wood is blocked, and follow the road round left then right at a junction. Just past the left hand bend at the entrance to Hill House Farm cross a stile on your

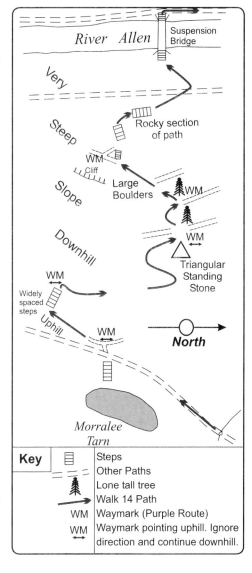

Key

	Steps	
	Other Paths	
	Lone tall tree	
	Walk 14 Path	
WM	Waymark (Purple Route)	
WM	Waymark pointing uphill. Ignore direction and continue downhill.	

right, almost concealed by a holly tree. Go slightly left over the crest of the hill to a fence. Follow this for half a mile to come to a road (the path does not seem to turn right as shown on the OS map). Turn right to Peelwell and right again to follow the road down into Haydon Bridge, (see Map for Walk 13) over (or preferably under) the A69, and down across the old bridge to the Anchor Inn.

Walk 15: Allen Banks to Willimoteswick & Shankfoot (circular)

A very pretty walk high above the river with views across to Hadrian's Wall returning past ancient Willimoteswick and pretty Beltingham. (This walk could also start/finish at Bardon Mill Station).

Time: *Allen Banks to Willimoteswick (circular) - 2½ hours, to Shankfoot (circular) - 3½ hours.*

Terrain: *Some country roads, fields, firm paths. Some stepping stones over streams, steps (can be avoided), 14 stiles, 1 kissing gate.*

Start: *Allen Banks National Trust car park.*

Go South out of the Allenbanks car park and either go about ¼ mile along the river bank and then climb the steep flight of steps on your right or very soon after leaving the car park take the orange waymarked right fork and follow that path to the top of the hill and continue to a waymarked stile on your right opposite the top of the flight of steps. Cross this and follow the edge of Ridley Hall grounds on an embankment. At a stile and gateway by a clump of trees there is a boggy area to cross before reaching a stile leading via a short farm lane to a road. Turn left and then right at the next junction where there is a phone box. About ¼ mile further on, just before a cottage, turn left up a farm road signposted 'Allensgreen 1' (it is in fact 2!). Follow this until it turns left towards woods. There is a waymarked stile on your right. Climb this and follow the excellently waymarked route over two more stiles and through a line of trees which leads up to Shaws Farm. Cross another stile at the trees' edge. Keep straight on to a stile beyond a second line of trees. Negotiate a small stream and cross the field to the left end of a wall leading down to ruined High Barn. Continue over two more stiles to a road. For the shorter walk turn right and follow this down to Willimoteswick. [*This name may derive from Guillemot's village – the furthest these birds ventured up the Tyne. A working farm, parts of the House, where Bishop Ridley the Martyr was born, are 11th century and the perimeter walls 13th*].

To continue to Shankfoot turn left, follow the road through a gate, over a small stream, and after crossing a waymarked (on the step) stile by a metal gate on your right go diagonally left across a field to its furthest corner to cross another stile onto a road. Turn right and continue to Allensgreen. Go through a gate avoiding the main house, but continuing, via two gates, through the farm buildings, then across a bridge over a stream. At the next gate, a clearly defined tractor track follows a fence on your right to a gate. Once through this some agility is needed to cross the Willimoteswick Burn, having done which you continue slightly left across the field aiming for a metal gate in the wall leading to the left hand end of a line of trees. Through the gate you turn right onto a farm track. Follow this through two gates, past the ruined High Barns, zigzagging down to join another farm road just before Shankfoot.

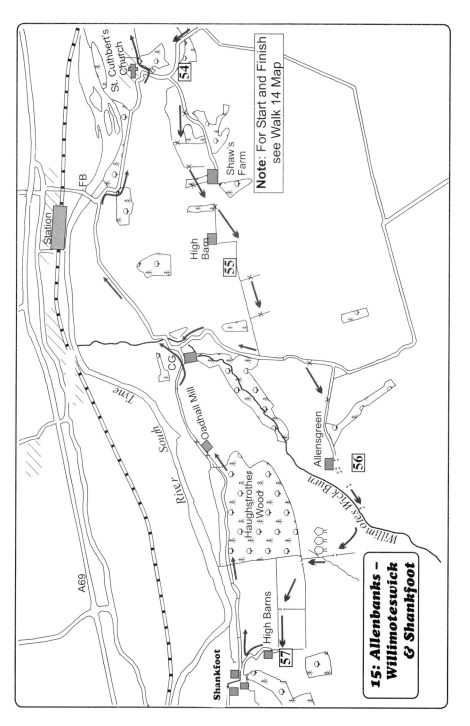

15: Allenbanks –
Willimoteswick
& Shankfoot

Note: For Start and Finish see Walk 14 Map

St. Cuthbert's Church

54

Shaw's Farm

High Barn

55

Station

FB

Tyne

South

River

A69

CG

Oadhall Mill

Haughstrother Wood

Allensgreen

56

Willimotes Wick Burn

High Barns

57

Shankfoot

To complete Walk 15 turn sharp right along this road as waymarked.

[If walking on to Haltwhistle continue left to Shankfoot through a gate, over a bridge, and right then left past the farm buildings to emerge onto Unthank Road. Continue along this pretty, little used road to Plenmeller and Haltwhistle – see Walk 16.

Walk 15 continues East along a clearly defined farm road through two gates to Haughstrother Wood, beyond which there are two stiles at Oadhall Mill. The road continues slightly uphill through a gate and over a cattle grid past Willimoteswick, where we meet the road and our shorter route. Continue along the road to Beltingham (though you can cross the river to/from Bardon Mill by the footbridge shown on the map).

[Beltingham Church – St. Cuthbert's – was built in the early 16th century. Three yew trees in the churchyard date back 2 centuries earlier. Part of the churchyard is reserved for the Bowes Lyon family. The late Queen Mother, Queen Elizabeth, planted a tree in the Churchyard. Look for a small black plaque].

Just past the church, at White Heather Cottage a sign points down a wide grassy path to 'Ridley Bridge ¾ Allen Banks 1½'. Take this path, which soon narrows beside a stream and comes to a kissing gate. Traverse this and, keeping a wire fence to your right, follow the path to the road. Turn left and at Ridley Hall gates turn right into the road that takes you back to the start at Allen Banks car park.

Walk 16: Haltwhistle – Plenmeller – Warren House (circular)

(If walking from Haydon Bridge or Bardon Mill you would join the walk at Plenmeller/Whitfield Road junction).

After easy roads leaving Haltwhistle, this becomes quite a rugged moorland walk for a couple of miles and only experienced walkers should attempt it in poor visibility, when you would anyway miss the splendid views from Warren House. To avoid road walking to/from Haltwhistle 2 or 3 cars could park where the South Tyne Trail joins Plenmeller Road.

> **Distance**: 4½ miles (7km)   To/from S. Tyne Trail/Plenmeller Rd - 3½ miles (5½km)
> **Time**: 2½ hours
> **Terrain**: Roads near Haltwhistle, farm tracks, rough moorland, 2 stiles.
> **Start**: Haltwhistle Railway Station or at Plenmeller Road

Turn right out of the station yard and almost at once go under the railway to cross the river. Turn left onto a road which takes you round to the A69. Cross this with care and go ahead up the Plenmeller road, where you will shortly pass the

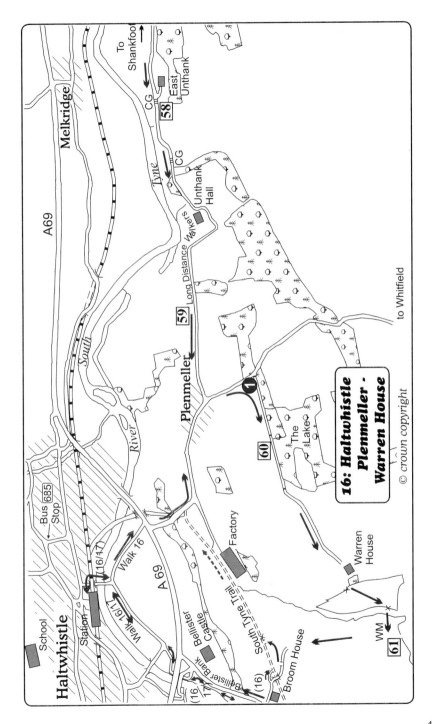

16: Haltwhistle - Plenmeller - Warren House

© crown copyright

Haltwhistle
School
Station
Bus 685 Stop
A69
Melkridge
A69
South River Tyne
To Shankfoot
East Unthank
CG
58
CG
Unthank Hall
Long Distance Walkers
59
Plenmeller
to Whitfield
60
The Lake
Walk 16(17)
Walk 16
Walk 16(1?)
Factory
Bellister Bank
Bellister Castle
South Tyne Trail
(16 17)
(16)
Broom House
Warren House
WM
61

start of the South Tyne Trail on your right. Continue on past the turn to Unthank, where walkers from Walk 15 would join this walk, up the hill towards Whitfield until you come to two metal gates on opposite sides of the road **(1)**. Go through the right hand gate and follow the farm track gradually uphill, through 2 gates pausing, perhaps to look down at the delightful lake on your left. At the gateway to ruined Warren House a waymark guides you right and then left across boggy, rocky moorland (paths are indistinct for the next 1½ miles) to a stile over a wall. Continue diagonally left downhill (aiming between two clumps of trees a couple of miles ahead) to a ladder stile, where a waymark suggests you go left. It is better in fact to go slightly right ahead over a boggy stream. About 100 yards ahead you should see a waymarked post which will advise you to turn right (i.e. North) uphill. As there is no path across the bumpy turf to this post, it is easier to follow one of the sheep (?) pathways going uphill from the stream. Providing you keep slightly West of North you will soon join the beaten track from the way marked post. Once Haltwhistle comes in sight, aim for the big modern school building on the left of the town, and your path joins the indistinct farm track, which once you are over the 'summit' becomes a clearly defined, if rough, approach to Broomhouse (To return to Plenmeller Road either go through a waymarked gate on your right as you descend towards Broomhouse and follow the track round right then down left to join the South Tyne Trail at a stile and a gate, or continue down to cross the railway bridge and turn right onto the trail). At the farm follow the waymark to the main road. Turn right and down the hill past Bellister Castle – for a closer look take the National Trust path over the stile halfway down the hill. You can join Walk 17 by turning left into the woods on Bellister Bank.

[*The castle dates from at least 1541. It has a ghost, the Grey Man, suspected by the Lord of Bellister of being a spy. The Lord set his bloodhounds on the man. They killed him and his aggrieved ghost returns from time to time*].

Bellister Castle

Just before the A69, take the path signposted 'Haltwhistle ½ mile', go under the main road (not across the river here) and alongside the river passing the road to Bellister Bridge. Continue along this road (South of the Tyne) until you come to the turning to the bridge you crossed at the start of the walk. Turn left to cross it and left on the far bank to return to the railway station.

Haltwhistle to Alston – Walks 17 to 22

When planning your walks bear in mind the very limited bus service between Haltwhistle and Alston, if you have no car. The South Tyne Trail is now open from the Plenmeller Road (Walk 16) to the source of the Tyne. It provides a direct all-weather route with the fascination of seeing at first hand the amount of engineering - cuttings, embankments, bridges, including the magnificent Lambley Viaduct - needed to build the original railway, most of it done by pickaxe, spade, horsedrawn wagon and wheelbarrow. From the Plenmeller Road to Featherstone it is also a hard surface cycleway. The trail cannot follow the river as closely as some of the paths, but it affords wide views for much of its length. It gives the long distance walker a choice of route. If you want to follow the river and like more rugged walking you should perhaps use the outward legs of Walks 17, 18 and 19, join the Trail at Whitwam (near mile [68]) and continue thence to Alston. If time is short then use the Trail all the way. Each of the six walks provides access to the Trail at some point so a third possibility is to make up your own route following a combination of the most interesting stretches of walk and Trail.

Distances: Haltwhistle to Alston. Maximum (excluding Walk 16) – 14½ miles (23km), minimum – using South Tyne Trail from Plenmeller Road to Alston – 12½ miles (20km).

Time: Experienced walkers know their own speed. Some of the non-trail sections would need more care and be a little slower. See individual walks for distances, time, terrain and car parking.

Refreshments: Pubs, cafés in Haltwhistle, Wallace Arms at Featherstone (Walk 17), Kirkstyle Inn (Walks 19/20), hotels, pubs, cafés in Alston.

Walk 17: Haltwhistle – Featherstone – Park Village (circular)

A very pretty walk above or beside the river as far as Featherstone, returning across fields and woodland, and along the South Tyne Trail.

Turn right out of the station yard and almost at once go right under the railway and across the river. Turn right into Bellister Road and continue under the A69 beside the river to emerge onto the Featherstone road. Turn right and up the hill. Look out for the signpost on the right 'Park Village 1 mile'. Go through a wicket gate to a sunken path. Follow this round to the right where it becomes a delightful cliff top path with occasional benches to afford a view of the river curving away below for

Distance: 6 miles (10 km), 5 miles (8km) from A69   **Time**: 3 hours

Terrain: Country roads, but mainly paths (care needed when high above the river) and fields. Steep flight of steps (can be avoided – see text), 17 stiles.

Refreshments: Haltwhistle and Wallace Arms – Featherstone

Car Parking: Street parking in Haltwhistle. Near A69 (see below). Featherstone station.

Start: Haltwhistle Railway Station – or there is space for a few cars opposite the entrance to Bellister Castle, just before the A69 junction over a cattle grid by signpost 'Haltwhistle ½' - Walk Maps on pages 46 and 51.

the next mile to North Wood. **The path is very narrow in places with steep drops on the right so great care is needed especially with children.** Snowdrops, foxgloves and a glade of silver birch border the path. Ignore a path off to the right and arrive at signposts. Do not follow the direction over the stile to 'Park Village ¾ mile', but keep right to follow the narrow 'Woodland Path to Burnfoot'. Continue over a ladder stile by a gate and across the edge of a field to a stile with a National Trust waymark to enter North Wood. After a muddy stretch slightly uphill by a fence, the path broadens and continues downhill to become a firm bridleway. You come out onto the road over a stile beside a gate at Burnfoot, beside the caravan site. Continue along the riverside road to Featherstone Bridge (long-distance walkers should continue ahead towards the castle). To continue Walk 17 cross the stone stile opposite the bridge ('Featherstone Rowfoot 1') and cross two fields by stiles to woods. A long steep flight of wooden steps takes you up through there to another stile leading to fields (to avoid the steps, you could continue from Featherstone Bridge by the road past the castle up to Featherstone Station). You now cross four fields, all linked by stiles and good waymarking. Two prominent trees beyond a gap between two lines of trees show the general direction. Cross the stile at the left hand edge of the wood bordering the last field and shortly turn right over a stile into the wood, continuing beside the garden of the old Featherstone Station house to go out via a stile onto the road. Turn left, and, almost at once left again onto the South Tyne Trail (a car park a few yards along the road provides another start/finish for this walk – and beyond that the Wallace Arms). After about ½ mile you have a choice of route. Either continue along the Trail (take care crossing main road), turn off left just after the Broomhouse Farm road bridge through a metal gate and up to and past the farm to the main road and right down Bellister Bank for Haltwhistle or take the path off left up to and through Park Village to the main road. Very shortly climb a stile, signposted "Haltwhistle 2 miles" across the road on your right, turn left over a ladder stile and take the path diagonally right across two fields to rejoin the road by a stile – almost opposite climb another stile, signed 'Haltwhistle 1½' and go diagonally right over the field to rejoin the outward route at the 'Park Village ¾' stile. Continue right down the path and roads to your start.

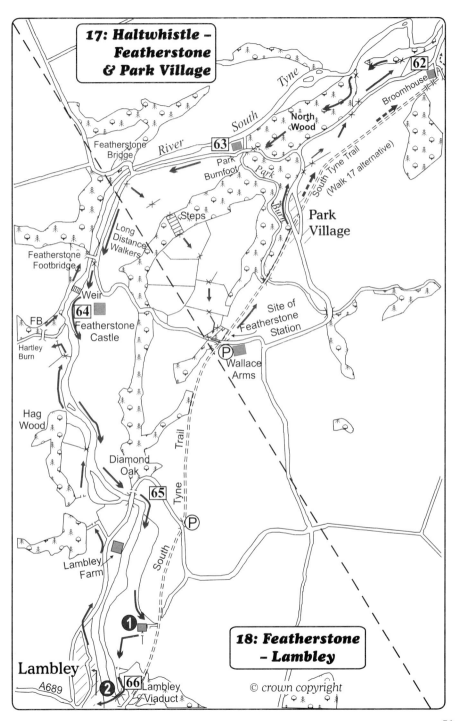

**17: Haltwhistle –
Featherstone
& Park Village**

South Tyne

River

North
Wood

62

Broomhouse

Featherstone
Bridge

63

Park
Burnfoot

South Tyne Trail
(Walk 17 alternative)

Steps

Park
Burn

Park
Village

Long
Distance
Walkers

Featherstone
Footbridge

Weir

64

Featherstone
Castle

FB

Hartley
Burn

Site of
Featherstone
Station

P

Wallace
Arms

Hag
Wood

Diamond
Oak

65

Trail

Tyne

P

Lambley
Farm

South

Tyne

Trail

1

**18: Featherstone
– Lambley**

Lambley

A689

2 66 Lambley
Viaduct

© crown copyright

Walk 18: Featherstone to Lambley (circular)

An undemanding and pretty walk through the grounds of Featherstone Castle, alongside the river to the magnificent Lambley Viaduct. Return through Lambley Village and along the other side of the river.

Distance: 4 miles (6½ km).   **Time**: 2 hours

Terrain: Firm paths, short stretches of road, fields, 5 stiles, steep steps up to Lambley.

Car parking: Lay-by at Featherstone Footbridge could fit a few cars

Start: Featherstone Footbridge (map on 49)

To the right of the road on the Castle side of the footbridge, follow the footpath sign 'Public Bridleway 300 yards, Public Footpath Diamond Oak 1' over a stile, turn left, and along good riverside path followed by a firm metalled bridleway to join the road at Diamond Oak.

Featherstone Castle

[Featherstone Castle certainly dates from 12th or 13th centuries. During the 1939-45 war it housed a Prep School and its grounds a POW camp, traces of which you can see approaching Diamond Oak. Featherstone, too, has its ghosts – a whole wedding party of them – when the Lord of the Manor (a Featherstonehaugh) forced his daughter to marry a husband of his choice, her jilted lover ambushed and killed the wedding party – including, accidentally, the bride. He then killed himself. All the murdered company are said to return to the castle on the anniversary of the wedding].

Cross the road and go through the two gates opposite, signed 'Coanwood ¾ mile'. Follow the track down to the riverside (path unclear), until you see a line of telegraph poles crossing the meadow, with a house **(1)** just below woods slightly to your left (almost 'ten o'clock'). Head away from the river to pass just to the left of this house, and cross a small stream on a log bridge. Ignore the rocky access road to your left, and turn sharp right behind the house at a gate. Continue ahead down a field with a steep drop as you near the further side, after descending which turn left

52

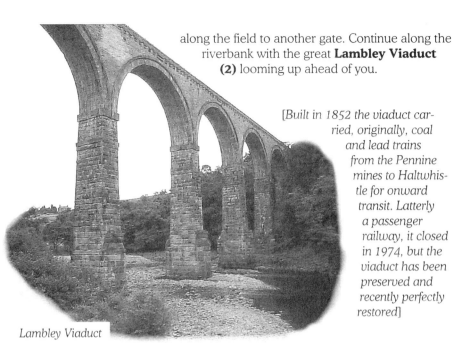

along the field to another gate. Continue along the riverbank with the great **Lambley Viaduct (2)** looming up ahead of you.

[*Built in 1852 the viaduct carried, originally, coal and lead trains from the Pennine mines to Haltwhistle for onward transit. Latterly a passenger railway, it closed in 1974, but the viaduct has been preserved and recently perfectly restored*]

Lambley Viaduct

Walk 18 continues across the footbridge on your right. The Long-distance walkers' route continues ahead, not over the footbridge, following Walk 19, though everyone is strongly recommended to cross the footbridge, turn left, and climb the steps to visit the viaduct and walk along it. Half-way up a signpost indicates the four routes, which radiate from this 'crossroads'. Walk 18 follows the Lambley village direction, up the remaining steps (1 counted 99 from the river). At the gate above stone steps turn right and follow a fence, with the trackbed of the old railway siding below you, behind the village to a wicket gate. Just past a cottage turn left and then right down the village street, continuing right, along the main road downhill to Lambley Farm. Turn left through a wicket gate down the farm track signposted 'Public Bridleway – Low Burnfoot 1 mile'. Pass through 2 gates and a stile, then over a field drain (very muddy here) into Hag Wood and up a short steep slope, keeping as near as you can to the fence on your right. Continue beside this fence protecting the top of the badly eroded riverbank. Cross another stile and keep alongside a fence to your left. At a gate turn left and follow a sandy, rocky stretch of path to cross a footbridge over Hartley Burn. Turn right, follow the path round left to the riverbank, passing the weir. Continue to the steps leading up to the footbridge, cross it, and return over the stile, to your starting point.

Walk 19: Lambley to Eals (circular)

This is a beautiful walk, but the most challenging in the book and inadvisable in very wet or icy conditions as the narrow uneven path has severe drops down to the riverside on some high stretches.

Distance: 3½ miles (6km)
Time: 1½ – 2 hours
Terrain: Fields, firm but difficult (in places) paths, return via South Tyne Trail. Steps, 6 stiles.

Refreshments: Kirkstyle Inn (1½ miles south of Eals)

Car Parking: Some roadside in Lambley Village or Coanwood on South Tyne Trail and walk the extra ¾ mile to the start along the Trail and over the viaduct.

Start: East end of Lambley footbridge, adjacent to the viaduct.

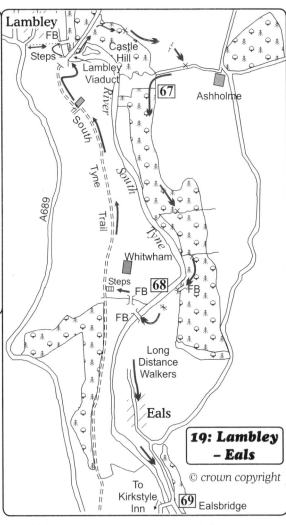

19: Lambley – Eals

© crown copyright

Turn towards the viaduct and follow the waymarked path under it and up to your left. The path climbs steeply towards the top of the viaduct and is sheer to one side before plunging down to the river again. Although the path appears to continue along the river bank, our route veers away left almost at once at the bend North of the island (see map) - look out for the widely placed wooden steps and follow them up to a T junction. Continue right about 200 yards until a left turn brings you to a stile leading out of Castle Wood into a field (if the path suffers further erosion beside the viaduct, it would be possible to retrace one's steps, go back over the footbridge, climb the steps and cross the viaduct going on to where a fence joins the trail at right angles, climb the section of fence parallel to the Trail and you will find a path which joins the walk route to the stile). Keep to the right hand edge of this field for a couple of hundred yards – splendid views of the viaduct through the trees – then veer diagonally left towards a waymarked gateway with Ashholme Farm on the hillside beyond. Go through the gateway and straight up to the top corner of the field where a ladder stile leads to a farm track. Turn right down this to the woods, which you enter through a gate. A few yards on, turn left (do not go on down the hill) along a pleasant (though muddy in winter) wide path through firs and, later, silver birch. After about half a mile cross a stile and a shallow stream. Do not go through an inviting gate to your right, but to the left of the ensuing wall – hoof marks have all but obliterated the path, so make your way along as near the line of the wall as is practicable until you come to another stream with a stile beyond. A wide ride stretches ahead but after only about 10 paces move off to the right to find a clearly defined but narrow path, which may be flanked by stretches of a single wire on the right – no waymarks here. Stay on this path as there are sheer cliffs out of sight below the steep slope to the right and care is needed on the path itself as it descends steeply to a footbridge over a small stream. Cross this and a stile and continue through fields beside the river and over a ladder stile to reach Eals footbridge.

[If walking to Alston ignore the bridge and carry straight on to join the farm road through Eals to Eals Bridge – others might like to go the further ¾ mile for sustenance at the Kirkstyle Inn (see Map Walk 20) before returning. The Inn is open midday (except Tuesdays) and every evening].

Cross the bridge and shortly bear right to another footbridge. Cross this, turn left and follow the stream with a slope on your right past a waymark up a short steep slope to steps, which take you onto the Trail. Turn right and walk back to Lambley, where you will have to descend to the river bank and back up again (for the village) to bypass the former station, now a private house.

Walk 20: Eals to Williamston and Slaggyford (circular)

Another very attractive, longer walk, climbing twice up the valley side for some wonderful views. Return partly on road (which is also, briefly, the Pennine Way) and partly along the South Tyne Trail. The Kirkstyle Inn (see Walk 19) provides refreshment ¾ mile from the finish.

At the East end of the bridge turn right, past a red mark and follow a metalled road which swings left then right at a junction to cross a bridge, through a gate and up through woods and two more gates to Bog Farm. Notice the waterfall (1) on the left to which a woodland path leads. Go through the waymarked gate with the Farm house on your left and, after you cross the farmyard, two more gates lead to a rocky track with a stone wall on your right. Where the wall turns right keep straight on along the now grassy track across the open hillside. When another track comes down from the hillside on your left look out for a waymark directing you downhill past a disued kiln and a larger ruin to a gate. Cross a stream on some long log-like

Distance: 5½ miles (9 km)
Time: 2½ hours
Terrain: *Some quiet roads (short stretches of main road), farm tracks, fields, 2 stiles*
Car Parking: *Plenty of space either end of Eals Bridge.*
Refreshments: *Kirkstyle Inn – open midday (except Tuesdays) and every evening*
Start: *Eals Bridge*

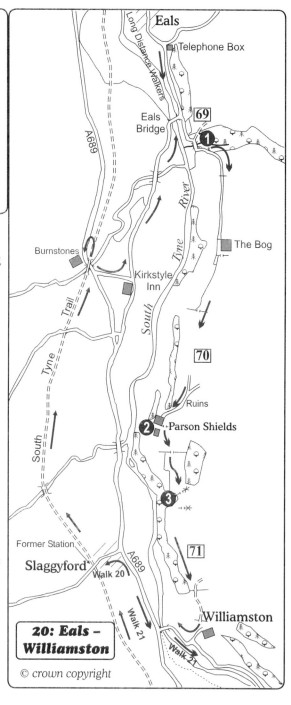

stone beams. Ahead is Parson Shields and an inviting gate. Avoid the invitation by turning left just before it and skirting a barn to a waymarked gate; beyond which, a little below you, is a cottage **(2)**. Turn left away from the cottage up a steep slope with a stream on the left. When a metal gate comes in sight ahead proceed through it towards a wooden gate which you ignore and keep to its left following the line of wire fence on your right (follow the waymark) until you come to 2 gates, one an unusual one with a frame on top labelled 'Keep Gate Closed' which leads through what seems a most attractive garden **(3)** with daffodils lining the path, though there is no house nearby. You emerge from the 'garden' through a similar gate/stile onto open hillside again. Veer slightly right then left to a line of telegraph poles. The path parallels a fenced wood about 20 yards to your right. At the end

56

of the wood the path tends downhill (and there are reassuring glimpses of Alston four miles ahead if the visibility is right). You join a rocky farm track at a metal gate. Continue down across to another farm gate leading into Williamston Farm. Note the date (1657) on the attractive farmhouse. Bear right along the farm road onto the 'main' road. Long-distance walkers should now turn left and join Walk 21. To continue Walk 20, turn right (straight ahead in fact) to follow the road onto the A689. Keep right along the roadside (you are also on the Pennine Way here), turn left into Slaggyford and up through the village to the old station where you turn right to join the South Tyne Trail. Continue for a mile and 100 yards after it crosses the A689 on a bridge at Burnstones turn left onto the main road and follow it back under the bridge you have just crossed on the Trail. Turn left down a side road to a T-Junction, turn right for the Kirkstyle Inn or left to follow the road back to Eals Bridge and your starting point.

Walk 21: Slaggyford to Kirkhaugh (circular)

Another pretty walk, which takes you above the river for some wonderful views up and down the valley. A half-way detour would be a ride on the South Tynedale Railway in the summer. You would need to check times in advance.

Turn right out of Slaggyford along the A689 (and, incidentally, the Pennine Way). Shortly turn left down the side road, over the river and continue along this road, where long distance walkers join this walk at the Williamston road end, for half a mile until it turns sharp left at a cattle grid. Turn off right at the sign 'Barhaugh Park', crossing Barhaugh Burn on a very high footbridge with a flight of steps at its far end. Turn left and then right round the edge of the wood and up a flight of mossy stone steps. Continue over the fields to the right of a large clump of trees and then to the left of a second clump up a steepish hill. Barhaugh Hall is to your left. Go over a stile onto a road, turn right and follow this for a short distance. At a former pumping station, a footpath sign directs you down to the right of a clump of trees (which seem to house the local rubbish dump). Keep in a leftish direction now along a reasonably clear path with woods on your right. Cross three ladder stiles and you will come to a wall from which the stones of the stile have disappeared. There is a convenient gate just to your left. Follow the road down towards Kirkhaugh (walkers to Alston, and anyone else who wishes a closer look at the attractive Church keep straight on). This walk turns nearly 180 degrees right where a farm track leaves the road. Go over a stile by a gate, follow the edge of the field round left to Kirkhaugh footbridge. There is a stone stile at the far end; cross it and go diagonally left up through trees and a field to another stile at the newly (2000) opened Kirkhaugh Station of the South Tyne Railway. Cross the stile and turn right. You are now on the South Tyne Trail, a narrow path. As it follows the line of the station fence it broadens at the overbridge where the railway line currently terminates.

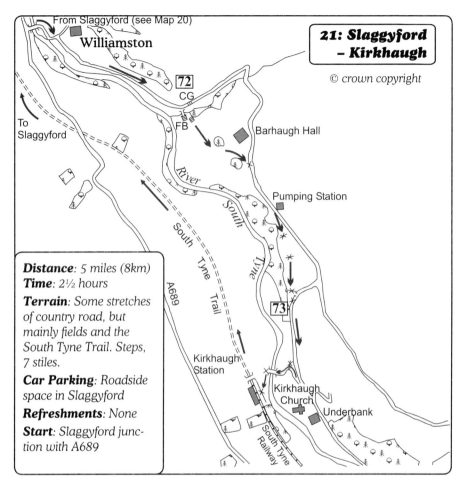

© crown copyright

Distance: 5 miles (8km)
Time: 2½ hours
Terrain: Some stretches of country road, but mainly fields and the South Tyne Trail. Steps, 7 stiles.
Car Parking: Roadside space in Slaggyford
Refreshments: None
Start: Slaggyford junction with A689

[When the standard gauge Haltwhistle to Alston Railway closed in 1974 efforts began to replace at least some of its length by a narrow gauge line. The line is now open throughout the Summer and at Christmas and Easter. Trains are hauled by preserved Steam and Diesel engines. There are many special events and the line is highly popular, especially with children. The original station at Alston provides tickets and information about this, England's highest railway. The South Tyne Trail continues beside the working railway.]

To complete the walk return to Slaggyford along the South Tyne Trail (see Map 20).

Walk 22: Kirkhaugh to Alston (circular)

An attractive but, apart from a steep hill at the start, an undemanding walk, which could, of course, equally well be done to/from Alston. Alston is worth exploring. With its cobbled main streets it is the highest market town in England and an excellent centre from which to explore the North Pennines ('England's last wilderness') and the former lead mining industry

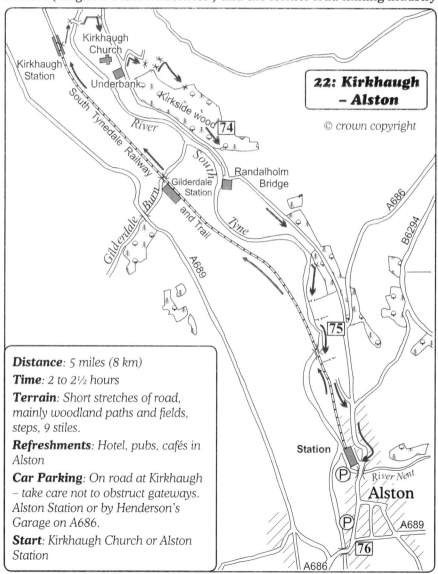

22: Kirkhaugh – Alston

© crown copyright

Distance: 5 miles (8 km)

Time: 2 to 2½ hours

Terrain: Short stretches of road, mainly woodland paths and fields, steps, 9 stiles.

Refreshments: Hotel, pubs, cafés in Alston

Car Parking: On road at Kirkhaugh – take care not to obstruct gateways. Alston Station or by Henderson's Garage on A686.

Start: Kirkhaugh Church or Alston Station

centred on nearby Nenthead and Upper Weardale (Killhope is well worth a visit too, as is nearby Allenheads in Northumberland).

Just south of the church turn left up a zigzag track signposted 'Bridleway'. At the second 'zig' (or 'zag') where the track turns left keep straight on diagonally left up a rough field to its top left hand corner. Cross the remains of a broken stone stile and keep left to come almost at once to two stiles between a wire fence, and the wall you have just crossed. Waymarks point ahead and right. Take the right hand direction following a wire fence bordering Kirkside Wood (partially felled in 2000). Cross a waymarked stile by a metal gate and follow a wide stone-based track down to gain the road, via a kissing gate, at Randalholm Bridge. Continue along the rising road for about half a mile to reach a metal signpost ('Footpath to Alston') on the right where the river bears away below you. Follow this rather slippery footpath, with occasional steps, down through woods to a stone stile. Cross this and follow the path with a wall on your right crossing three fields through gates to pass a cottage on your right. Its approach track leads to the A686. Follow this along to the right and after a sharp right hand bend turn down to the station, or, if this is your final destination continue into the town. Cross the level crossing and turn right onto the footpath beside the line and follow this, the South Tyne Trail (or be lazy and catch a train!) to Kirkhaugh Station. Leave the platform by a stile on the right, go diagonally left downhill to a stone stile, cross this and the footbridge over the river. Follow the near edge of the field left and right, then turn right by a gate and stile onto the road and ahead to Kirkhaugh Church.

Walk 23: *Alston to Garrigill (circular)*

A very pretty walk high above the river, and crossing the beautiful Nattrass Gill as far as Bleagate, with extensive moorland views including Cross Fell, the highest point of the Pennines. After Bleagate the walk continues to Garrigill along the river bank, with plenty of scope for picnics and for children to play.

As the outward and return routes cross at Bleagate two shorter circular walks are possible: Alston to Bleagate, Garrigill to Bleagate (see map - page 63).

Turn right out of the station **(1)**, then right again onto the A686 and shortly left up the steep, cobbled A689 through the town centre. Follow the road round to the right, still uphill. At the top of the hill take the narrow road between the 'Swan's Head' **(2)** and the Wesleyan Chapel **(3)** signposted 'Nattrass Gill / High Nest'. At a similar sign continue ahead along a metalled path between stone walls with new housing on your left, to come to another 'Nattrass Gill' direction sign, where you turn left, immediately right and straight ahead through 2 gates at Fairhill and along the farm track to Annat Walls. Go through 2 gates – boggy hereabouts. Two more stiles (waymarked) bring you alongside a wire fence, with a steep drop beyond,

Distance: *Alston to Garrigill and return 9 miles (14½ km). The Bleagate alternatives are 4 miles (6 ½ km) from/to Alston, 5 miles (8 km) from/to Garrigill.*

Time: *4 ½ hours*

Terrain: *Short stretches of road and farm tracks, mainly firm paths and fields, some muddy patches and steep flight of steps at Nattrass Gill. 44 stiles.*

Public Transport: *Very sparse to/from Alston to anywhere. Essential to consult up-to-date timetables: virtually none to Garrigill.*

Refreshments: *Hotels, pubs, cafes in Alston, Teas at Thortergill and Garrigill Post Office, George & Dragon at Garrigill.*

Car parking: *Alston Station, roadside elsewhere and at Garrigill.*

Start: *Alston Station* **(1)**

leading into the wooded defile of Nattrass Gill. Go down steps across a footbridge over a waterfall up further steps to a second footbridge over a side stream then out across a wooden stile and left (waymarked) round what looks like a cricket field with High Nest beyond. Cross a field by stone and metal stiles onto a road, turn left and then right at the junction – signpost 'Bleagate'. At Woodstock turn right past the front of the house to a field gate. You may have to detour right of a boggy patch to reach the stile in the wall opposite. Pass through a thin belt of woodland and then follow the waymark direction diagonally right across a field, through another strip of woodland, over a stone stile across a field to a gate opposite, leading, into Bleagate farmyard [If the ground is very wet you could, of course, do the Woodstock – Bleagate section by road]. Turn right down in front of the farm house.

Alston

61

If returning to Alston go over the waymarked stone stile to the left of the gate ahead and turn right then follow directions for last section of the main walk (below). To continue to Garrigill turn left after the farm house, through a metal gate, and at the end of a breeze block farm building on your left turn sharp right downhill, over a stile en route to a concrete based bridge over the river. Cross this and turn left over a footbridge flanked by stiles along the riverside path, which traverses an area of uprooted (by floods?) trees then a rocky 'beach' before crossing fields via a series of footbridges, gates and stiles. At the next footbridge (don't cross it) over the Tyne you join the Pennine Way, clearly waymarked over further stiles past Middle Skydes and up a short slope to cross a stone stile and continue beside a wall on top of a bank some 50 yards from the river. The next stile takes you along the edge of a spoil heap and a small timber yard to join a farm track leading onto a road. The delightful hamlet of Garrigill is well worth continuing along the road to visit, and long distance walkers would continue there anyway, but if you are short of time, turn left once you are out onto the road at a signpost "Public Footpath to Baldy Chapel" and cross the footbridge over the river, turn right and follow the path beside a wall, keeping leftish at Garrigill Burn and uphill to join the road opposite Thortergill (see page 63). Turn left and follow the directions below.

Walkers to the Source of the Tyne continue from Garrigill on Walks 24 and 25.

[**Crossfell**: *Shortly beyond Garrigill the Pennine Way continues South-westwards to the summit of Crossfell, a linear walk of 14 miles (22 ½ km) there and back. Easy walking, but beware, in this whole area, of unprotected old lead mining shafts if you leave the beaten track.*]

To return to Bleagate and Alston, cross Garrigill Bridge and turn sharp left along the road past Thortergill until you come to the cemetery at the far end of which follow the 'Bleagate' sign through a gate on your left and diagonally right across a field and through a gap between walls. Now follow the wall on your right to a footbridge over a pretty tree-lined stream with a succession of waterfalls. Leave the trees and cross 8 stone stiles (some of them just gaps over a step), which bring you to Low Craig. Continue through a gap between two walls to a pair of stiles with a ruined building **(4)** on your right. Follow the well waymarked path along the line of the wall and fence to your left over four stone 'gap' stiles to a waymarked wicket gate at the (ruined) Low Sillyhall. Follow the Bleagate direction at the three-armed sign-post "Pennine Way", up over a broken wall (very muddy hereabouts), turn slightly left then continue diagonally up the hillside and over a stile in the wall ahead then ahead to a metal gate and on to the gate taking you into Bleagate Farmyard. Turn left in front of the house and then right over the stone stile by a gate for the last lap back to Alston. You are now back on the Pennine Way, which follows the side of the hill above the river, alongside a wall (on your right) over a stile with a gate on top, through 2 gaps in walls ahead, over another stile and passing in front of Low Cowgap. Two more stone stiles and a gap in a wall take you past a tree-filled hollow to Low Nest. Skirt the garden wall, continue through a wall gap to a footbridge, flanked by two stiles, crossing Nattrass Gill and almost at once climb another stile

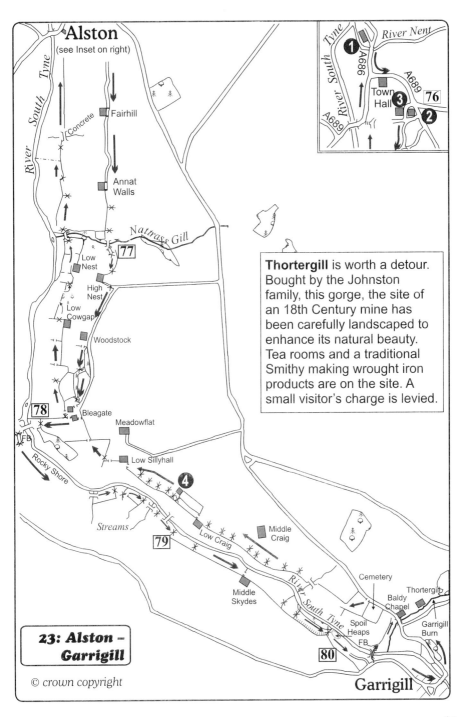

Alston
(see Inset on right)

River South Tyne

Concrete

Fairhill

Annat Walls

Natrass Gill

77

Low Nest

High Nest

Low Cowgap

Woodstock

78

FB

Bleagate

Meadowflat

Rocky Shore

Low Sillyhall

4

Streams

79

Low Craig

Middle Craig

Middle Skydes

River South Tyne

Cemetery

Thortergill

Baldy Chapel

Spoil Heaps

FB

Garrigill Burn

80

Thortergill is worth a detour. Bought by the Johnston family, this gorge, the site of an 18th Century mine has been carefully landscaped to enhance its natural beauty. Tea rooms and a traditional Smithy making wrought iron products are on the site. A small visitor's charge is levied.

River South Tyne

River Nent

1

A686

Town Hall

3

A689

76

2

A689

23: Alston – Garrigill

© *crown copyright*

Garrigill

63

into a field. Move down towards the wall on your left, follow it over two more stiles, and where it turns left continue ahead alongside a fence on your right, which after you have crossed the remains of a broken wall, becomes a wall. Follow this to a stone stile on your right, and cross a stream by some stone 'planks'. Ahead is a wide firm path, which takes you the rest of the way to Alston high above the river, though you can drop down and follow the waters edge by a side path. Just above the A686 river bridge the path meets a road near a Pennine Way information board. Turn left down steps to a roadside wall, in which to your left is a gap. Go through this, turn right and continue to the starting point.

Walk 24: Garrigill to Hole House (circular)

On Walks 24/25 the route from Garrigill to the source of the Tyne is well signposted 'South Tyne Trail' and waymarked clearly.

This very attractive, but not difficult, walk takes you almost to the last inhabited dwellings in the South Tyne valley with the moors all around you. You follow the impressive river gorge, much used by wet-suited gorge walkers. A short detour will take you to lovely Ashgill Force. It is possible, though at times risky, to walk behind the falls for dramatic views through the curtain of water.

Turn left and continue left along the road to Crossgill (about ½ mile). Just before the farm turn left down the farm lane (signposted 'South Tyne Trail Tynehead') and cross Windshaw Bridge. Turn immediately right and through a kissing gate into fields. The path follows the course of the river in and out of stretches of gorge. Cross two stone stiles at the second of which the path is confined between a fence and the river gorge. Just before the confluence with Ashgill turn left over a wooden stile and up beside the Gill to reach a four-armed signpost ('Garrigill, Low Crossgill, Ashgill, Tynehead'). Before turning right towards Tynehead the 15 minute detour to Ashgill is strongly recommended. [Cross the stile immediately ahead, continue through a wicket gate and a clear path leads you the rest of the way.] To continue Walk 24 proceed over the footbridge and through the gate at the far end. Climb a short distance up the bank below Birds Nest to turn right onto the wide track round the side of the hill to a low waymarked fence, which you cross. Waymarking is clear all the way now to Hole House. Pass a covered-in shaft on your right and onto a grassy farm track with a mainly firm stone base, though there are some boggy patches. Continue along this track through 3 gates to a small stream at which the track stops. Cross the stream and a stile at the top of a short bank. The path contin- ues now alongside the river. The ground is quite boggy and you cross a couple of small streams. Go through a metal gate (waymarked) and follow the fence on your right to Hole House. At a second metal gate turn left and follow the wall a short distance to cross a South Tyne Trail waymarked stone stile. Turn right and continue round a long farm building turning left past the farm house, then right over a bridge and up to the Garrigill Road (a footpath sign points back whence you have come to

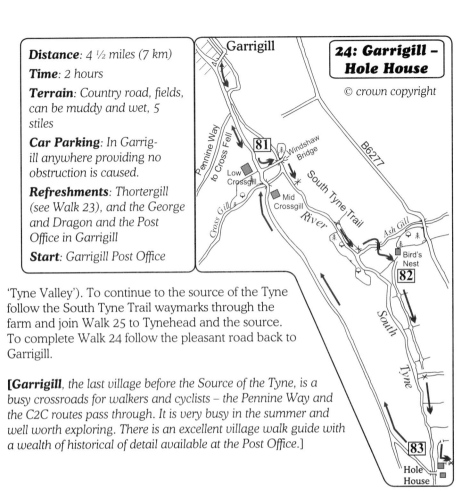

Distance: 4 ½ miles (7 km)

Time: 2 hours

Terrain: Country road, fields, can be muddy and wet, 5 stiles

Car Parking: In Garrigill anywhere providing no obstruction is caused.

Refreshments: Thortergill (see Walk 23), and the George and Dragon and the Post Office in Garrigill

Start: Garrigill Post Office

24: Garrigill – Hole House

© crown copyright

'Tyne Valley'). To continue to the source of the Tyne follow the South Tyne Trail waymarks through the farm and join Walk 25 to Tynehead and the source. To complete Walk 24 follow the pleasant road back to Garrigill.

[**Garrigill**, the last village before the Source of the Tyne, is a busy crossroads for walkers and cyclists – the Pennine Way and the C2C routes pass through. It is very busy in the summer and well worth exploring. There is an excellent village walk guide with a wealth of historical of detail available at the Post Office.]

Walk 25: Hole House to the Source of the Tyne

The extension of the South Tyne Trail southwards from Hole House using a permissive path from Tynehead onwards enables the first part of this walk to be circular, though the final 1½ miles to the source is a there-and-back walk [though long-distance walkers could do the 18 mile round from Garrigill, continuing on from the source across the Tees and up Troutbeck to join the Pennine way over Great and Little Dun Fell, Cross Fell and back to Garrigill. This would be a superb moorland walk with wonderful views of the Eden Valley and the Lake District].

As I followed the final 3 miles of the South Tyne I found it fascinating to see how soon the broad stream becomes a rivulet, and then to see the tiny hillside spring from where it starts. Moving too, I felt, to continue the mile or so to the Tees, and look up towards Burnhope Fell to the North East where the Wear rises – our three

Distance: *5 miles (8 km) 4 ½ miles (7 km) if omitting Hole House*

Time: *2½ or 2 hours*

Terrain: *Private road and some rough walking initially. Boots are advisable in case you wish to explore the various little tributaries. Take care though as dangerous mine shafts may still be open off the beaten track. 7 stiles*

Car Parking: *Anywhere along the ½ mile of road between the Hole House approach road and the 'limit of car travel' where you can find a stretch of verge without causing obstruction. No parking is allowed any further South than the cattle grid as the road is private thereafter.*

Refreshments: *None*

Start: *At the end of the public road running South from Garrigill or where you have parked.*

great North East rivers all within 5 miles of each other.

Walk North from your parking place to the Hole House approach road, turn right down it and across the river. Turn left and then right along the North side of a long new farm building. Go through a gate ahead of you and almost at once turn right over a stone stile with the distinctive blue 'S' shaped South Tyne Trail waymark. The route is thereafter clearly marked and signposted (South Tyne Trail) to Tynehead and onto the source. Continue over two stiles beside the river and then at Tynehead right through a wicket gate and left across a footbridge over a tributary stream.

[For the shorter walk, take the "Yad Moss" signpost direction at the end of the public road and follow the farm track downhill to Tynehead, cross the river and the stretch

Near the source of the River Tyne

already described at the footbridge]. At once turn left and through a metal gate then scramble up right over the remains of a ruined house. Follow a rough farm track past several remains of this once thriving village. Follow waymarks, roughly parallel to and above the river to a stile over a fence beside a gate. Cross this and follow the fence line on your right. You soon come to a second stile over the fence. Cross this and follow the fence (on your left) to cross it again at a third stile to avoid a steep drop to the river. Just past the waterfalls negotiate a fourth stile over the fence and where the fence turns left continue ahead and follow the

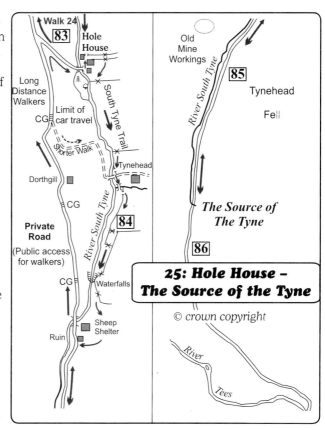

25: Hole House – The Source of the Tyne

The Source of The Tyne

© crown copyright

waymarks round the slope above the sheep shelter and down to the road beside a ruined building. The shelter enables sheep to be fed and protected in the winter snows. The road continues steadily uphill with the river on your right and the road becoming slatey. Off to the right is an old mine working. Suddenly the river changes from a 2 or 3 yard wide stream to a narrow rivulet running amid marsh. Indeed you could imagine it had disappeared altogether and two little tributaries rising to the left of the road from springs in the hillside and passing under the road could be mistaken for sources, but a wary few steps into the marsh enable you to hear the gurgle of the river still running down hill. Finally you come to a wide pipe under the road, through which the river starts its flow from hillside springs now commemorated by the handsome stone sculpture erected in March 2002. This is the source – you have completed walking the Tyne.

You may wish to continue to the Tees (see below), if not, retrace your steps to the start, crossing the river at the sheep shelter and following the road uphill over 2 cattle grids and past the now deserted Dorthgill to arrive back onto Garrigill Road.

'**Tynehead**': Various springs have been nominated as the source of the Tyne, but the commemorative sculpture favours the most generally accepted spot. Unlike Teeshead (OS Map Ref: 703339), which does seem to mark the source of that river, the only two map references to Tynehead (764380 & 765356) do not fulfill that function. The river does, of course, start on Tynehead Fell, but that is a large area. The building marked Tynehead is 2 miles from the source. This Tynehead incidentally was an important village 2 centuries ago, with its own Mayor.

The commemorative sculpture at the source of the River Tyne

The Tees: At the time of writing the Tees does not have the benefit of paths allowing the exploration of its upper reaches, so once you have completed the Tyne Walk, you might like to go on a mile or so and catch a glimpse of the Tees, with its impressive backdrop of Great and Little Dun Fells and Cross Fell. I was strangely moved to feel I could visit two of the North's great rivers within the space of 30 minutes.